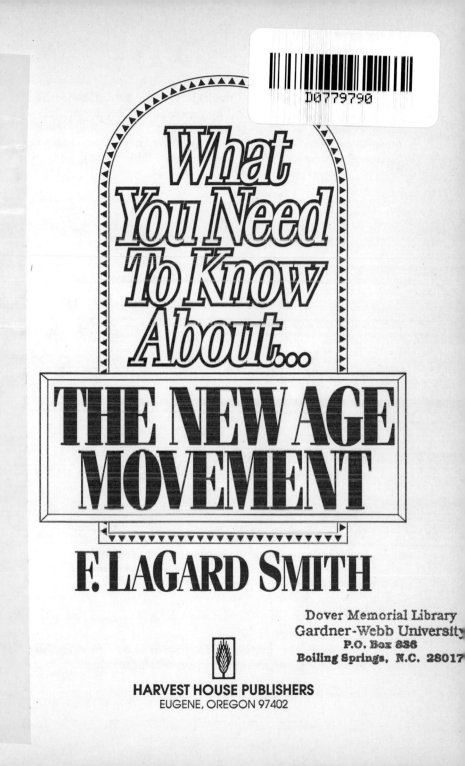

What You Need To Know About...

THE NEW AGE MOVEMENT

F. LaGard Smith

HARVEST HOUSE PUBLISHERS
EUGENE, OREGON 97402

WHAT YOU NEED TO KNOW ABOUT THE NEW AGE MOVEMENT

Copyright © 1993 by Harvest House Publishers
Eugene, Oregon 97402

Library of Congress Cataloging-in-Publication Data

Smith, F. LaGard (Frank LaGard), 1944–
    What you need to know about the New Age movement / F. LaGard Smith.
        p.   cm.—(Conversations with the cults)
    ISBN 1-56507-124-7
    1. New Age movement—Controversial literature.   2. Occultism—
Controversial literature.   3. Occultism—Religious aspects—
Christianity.   4. Christianity and other religions.   5. New Age
movement—Psychological aspects—Case studies.   6. Occultism—
Psychological aspects—Case studies.   I. Title.   II. Series.
BP605.N48S653   1993
    239'.9—dc20   93-7345
                                                                          CIP

Printed in the United States of America.

To my precious bride, Ruth,
as we begin
our journey together
in the pursuit of
love, laughter, and
a shared faith in Christ.

With Appreciation
to
Kimberly Logan
whose experiences and insight
made this book possible.

And to
Ray Oehm, my co-laborer
in the arduous endeavor of Christian writing,
whose keen eye has pored over every word
of my many manuscripts
and, as if in an act of Creation itself,
brought order out of chaos.

CONTENTS

———— ◆ ————

1

◆

Flying into the Flame

Sara had always been a believer. But now her faith was struggling. At 25, she was caught up in that maelstrom of confusion that comes to many young professionals: just out of college, unsure of her career, and—most of all—feeling the hurt of a failed relationship. In fact, *many* failed relationships.

Sara's insecurity and fear became the backdrop to a hellish year of struggling for personal identity and spiritual peace. Why else did she, a devout Christian, find herself going to a psychic? It wasn't just any storefront in the neighborhood strip mall that she was entering. It was what she had always been taught to be the domain of divination, evil spirits, and perhaps the devil himself. Had she lost all fear of Satan?

As she opened the door, a tiny bell on the push bar rang in Sara's ears. So did the ominous words of her mother: "Psychics are from the devil." Sara stepped determinedly forward, as if bold defiance would somehow justify what she was doing. Besides, her friends who had told her about going to psychics had never encountered the devil face-to-face. Quite to the contrary, psychics had told them personal aspects of their lives that they had never before shared with anyone. And with so many questions on her mind, it was this kind of insight that Sara desperately needed in her life.

"What do I have to lose?" Sara had asked herself earlier that afternoon. "If it's just a gimmick, then I'm out 20 dollars and no harm done. But if it works... there's no telling what I might gain." Besides, what harm could a simple tarot card reading do? Is there anyone whose curiosity doesn't prompt him or her to read the message inside the fortune cookie?

A plainly dressed dark-haired woman, middle-aged with slightly Oriental features, greeted Sara and introduced herself as Tina. "How may I help you?" Tina asked with an air of genuine concern. Sara told her that she was interested in a tarot card reading. "Have you consulted the tarot cards before?" Tina inquired. "No," said Sara, "but some of my friends have." Then Tina explained how the cards, each bearing certain traditional allegorical figures, were used in gaining knowledge about a person's life.

Something in Tina's voice captured Sara's confidence, but to break the ice she asked nervously, "Are you what some people would call a fortune-teller?" Tina laughed. "No, I'm a spiritual healer. I'm afraid I don't even own a crystal ball. And I assure you I don't have a broom or any witches' brew in the back room. What I do is to pray with my clients and teach them how to meditate. Depending upon what spiritual healing might be advisable, sometimes I might suggest participation in certain rituals. But generally I work with astrology and other traditional psychic tools such as the tarot cards to explore with you the questions you might have about the past, present, or even the future."

Sara liked the understanding way that Tina looked at her when she talked. Tina's eyes were dark and mysterious, as if she truly were in touch with the secrets of the universe. Yet one small seeming inconsistency did catch Sara off guard. It was that word *pray*. How odd, Sara thought, that a psychic would involve herself in prayer. Prayer seemed to belong to the world of the church, not to psychics.

While Tina walked over to a table to get the tarot cards, Sara quickly surveyed the room. It was filled with both the expected and the surprising. A heavy fragrance of incense hung over the room, just as one might expect. There were candles, too, and a bust of Buddha next to some wizards and unicorns. On the wall was a chakra chart   giving colors and descriptions of various parts of the body that are thought to be psychically significant—and a picture of a large eye that always seemed to be watching you.

But on a shelf containing New Age books on reincarnation, astral projections, and horoscopes was also what looked to be a well-thumbed Bible. Even more surprising was the faded picture of the Last Supper with Jesus and his disciples, and next to it a picture of the Virgin Mary.

Before Sara could further analyze the conflicting religious and philosophical streams which that eclectic scene implied, Tina was ready to go to work.

"Hold these cards in your hands and shuffle them," Tina instructed. "While you are doing that, I want you to make two silent wishes, one for yourself and one for someone you love. The wishes must not involve any monetary gain."

What would she wish for herself? Sara wondered. And for whom would she wish the second wish? Sara concentrated hard on both questions. The first wish was easier than the second. What she wished most for herself was a peace about her relationships with men.

At the time, Sara was dating someone new. Already the relationship was complicated, confusing, and exhausting. Although she was strongly attracted to Bob, things were not turning out the way she had hoped. She was pretty sure that Bob was dating other women behind her back, and naturally that thought set Sara on a roller coaster of mixed emotions. Sara wondered to herself if she would ever experience with a man the love and trust that she yearned for.

"Have you made your wishes?" Tina interrupted.

"I've made one," Sara responded, "but the second is more difficult."

Tina took the cards from Sara and looked at them intently. "There is a great deal of pain in your life," Tina began slowly. "You were not meant to go through such pain." But, Tina went on to explain, the pain was due to circumstances over which Sara had no control. It had nothing to do with Sara herself.

"Does it have anything to do with my boyfriend?"

"What is his name?"

"Bob. His name is Bob."

Tina then told Sara that the cards revealed a difficulty in their relationship. It was not Sara's fault, but Bob's. Bob's life was in chaos.

That much Sara knew to be true. Bob was struggling with his career as an actor. As long as that struggle continued, he was not likely to settle into any relationship.

"Bob is trying to find his balance, and you are only an innocent bystander," Tina assured Sara.

"The cards are very clear, Sara. This difficulty will not last forever. Bob is your soul mate. You are meant to be together. It is God's will."

Sara resisted that thought. Although she liked Bob a lot, she could never think of him as a soul mate. There had been too much conflict and too little trust.

Tina sensed Sara's skepticism. "Do you not think Bob is your soul mate?"

"I'm not sure, but I wouldn't think so."

"That would surprise me," said Tina, "because the cards are unusually clear that you know him as your soul mate. If it's not Bob, do you have any idea who your soul mate might be?"

Sara thought for a moment and wondered to herself whether it might be her ex-boyfriend James.

Tina ended the first half of the session, saying that she would meditate on this aspect of Sara's life for their next meeting. At Tina's request, Sara gave her three names to meditate over: Bob, James, and Adam (a man Sara had once dated for a couple of years).

Because Tina had focused in on Bob rather than James, Sara found herself wondering if Tina hadn't just been guessing. After all, Sara herself had supplied the names. All Tina had to do was to make up something about Sara's various boyfriends.

But even that doubt was quickly swept away. Tina returned to the pain in Sara's life which Tina had first seen in the cards. In some detail, she began to spell out incidents in Sara's childhood where Sara had felt spiritually attacked. "How could Tina possibly know about *those* instances?" Sara asked herself breathlessly.

For the first time in her life, Sara felt that someone saw what she had known her whole life. Incident by incident, Tina was affirming her private childhood fears. Just as she had always felt, those fears were real! And if *they* were real, how could Tina's contact with the realm of the supernatural be unreal?

At the end of the hour, Tina said that nothing in Sara's life could be balanced until her love life was settled. The cards had said that she was supposed to be with her soul mate now, and that something evil was keeping them apart. When Tina said she wanted to perform a ritual with crystals in order to heal Sara's chakras, Sara trusted her. They agreed to meet again three days later, and in the meantime each would meditate on who might be Sara's soul mate. Just before Sara left, Tina took Sara's hands in her own and prayed for Sara's healing.

With this first meeting, Sara's opinion of psychics had changed. Much to her surprise, they didn't reject God after all. Instead of being evil, they seemed to be working *with* God. How could psychics be from Satan when they believed in Jesus, and even prayed?

After just one brief meeting with Tina, Sara's life was about to take a dramatic turn. Would she find enlightenment in the flickering flame of Tina's scented candles, or would she instead find herself flying dangerously close to a deadly flame set alight by Satan himself?

2

◆

In Search of a Soul Mate

Sara could think of nothing else during the next two days. She could hardly wait to discover who her soul mate was. Surely, whoever it was would be the answer to all her questions and the key to her future. For hours at a time she sat on the floor in the lotus position with her legs crossed, meditating. Her room had been transformed into one resembling Tina's. There was sandalwood incense and mood music in the background. Meditation for Sara was an uncomplicated exercise. Instead of chanting some particular mantra, she sat in silence. At first her mind concentrated, then darted, then dreamed.

Sara relived vivid memories of Adam, Bob, and James—playing them over and over like a well-worn videotape. Which one was her true love, her soul mate? In her heart she knew.

— ◆ —

Sara was 15 minutes early for her next appointment. Tina greeted her warmly, like an old friend, and the two began to talk about the subject of their mutual meditations. Sara was absolutely bursting with expectation!

"Let me say, first of all, Sara, that you were right when you questioned the cards at the first session. Bob is not your soul mate. The cards were clear about Bob, but I may have been too anxious to unite the two of you in my own mind. What they were clear about was that Bob could fulfill you on many levels. Unfortunately, you and Bob are not spiritually compatible."

Sara was not at all surprised at that information. She and Bob had always had great fun together and an immediate affinity with each other. But Bob was not on her spiritual wavelength. His values were not hers, nor did he truly listen to her whenever she spoke from the depths of her soul. No, Bob could never be her soul mate. Tina was one for one.

"As for Adam," Tina began again, "my meditations tell me that the two of you were never meant for each other. Definitely not! He has inhibited you artistically and kept you from truly expressing yourself."

Sara flinched visibly. The analysis was perfect! In the two years they dated, Adam had always been overpossessive and insecure in their relationship. Once when she had written a screenplay as part of a drama class, Adam had read the script and laughed at her for submitting "such childish drivel," as he put it. Sara suspected that Adam was simply envious of her talent and was forced to put her down in order to bolster his own insecurity. Even so,

Adam's derision had hurt Sara deeply, and she had never again attempted to do any creative writing. There was no question about it: Adam was certainly not her soul mate. Tina was two for two! That left only James. Sara could hardly contain herself. From the very beginning, and throughout the long hours of meditation over the past two days, James had been the only one who could truly be her soul mate. Sara held her breath.

"I'm so happy you came to me, Sara," Tina began slowly. "What I am about to tell you is going to change your life completely. There is no question but that your soul mate is James."

Sara's face relaxed at the very sound of his name. A chill of confirmation went throughout her whole body as she leaned forward to hear more.

"James will fulfill you on every level—emotionally, intellectually, spiritually, sexually. You are destined by God to be together. Yours is a love for the ages."

Sara's whole body warmed with excitement.

"James loves you deeply, but for the moment there is someone standing between you and James," Tina cautioned. "I can't really tell who it is, but another woman is keeping you apart. This woman is destroying James, clouding his own clarity and draining vital spiritual energy away from you. Do you know who this woman is?"

Sara knew exactly who it was. But it was a long story. She told Tina how she had met James when the two of them were working in the same department store. Working together practically every day, they had quickly become good friends. When she first met James, he was seriously involved with a woman by the name of Diana whom he had dated off and on for four years. At first it hardly mattered, since Sara herself was still dating Adam. But then Adam and Sara broke up, and one week later James and Diana broke up. Because they were already attracted to each other, James and Sara started dating immediately.

Sara had never felt such an immediate sense of ease with a man. Rarely had any man in her past even turned her head, much less her heart. But James was different. When they went out to dinner for the first time, Sara had an incredible feeling of déjà vu. It was as if they had known each other forever. Sara had always believed that such instant feelings were only the stuff of romance novels. But how could she deny the way she felt? It was so real, so wonderful, so . . . right.

But barely a month had passed before Sara's dream romance came crashing to the ground. One day on a work break, James suddenly announced that he was getting back together with Diana. "I have been falling in love with you at the same time that I still love Diana," he lamented. "I just can't handle the fact that I'm feeling so strongly for two different women at the same time."

Sara was devastated. And yet in a strange way she was also relieved. Over the past month she had been so swept away by her love for James that the flood of emotions had at times been scary. Certainly she was in pain, but mostly confused. How could she have been so wrong about James?

Naturally it was difficult for Sara to keep working side by side with James. Petty squabbles arose at work, and their once-solid friendship simply couldn't survive. Sara eventually quit her job and moved to the other side of town to be completely away from James' world. She had no further contact with him for a time, and had begun to accept the fact that they would never be together again.

As Tina listened to Sara's story, she assured Sara that the initial feelings she had on their first date were true. She and James *had* known each other for more than that six months. In fact, they had known each other in at least one other lifetime!

That thought caught Sara off guard, for the implication was clear enough: In order for her to believe Tina's statement, she would have to believe in reincarnation, something she had always been taught to reject. How could a Christian like herself believe that everyone has lived many lifetimes? For the moment, however, Sara was clinging desperately to every word. What Tina was saying was of immense importance to Sara's achieving a peace about her life.

"In my meditations I saw quite clearly that you and James had been together hundreds of years ago, and—you must trust me on this—you were kept apart even then by the same entity. If you say that this woman is Diana today, then it was the same Diana in your previous life."

"How was she keeping us apart?" Sara asked with eager curiosity.

"It seems that in an earlier life, James had been married to Diana. But it is very clear that you were James' true love at the time you shared life together on the planet. Unfortunately, you yourself were not willing to reciprocate his love—or perhaps you were unable to, since James was in a lower economic

23

caste than yourself. At that time one's economic class was considerably more important than in our own time."

"Am I being punished in some way for rejecting James?"

"Quite possibly so. That's the way karma works. When you do something good, it rewards you. When you do something bad, you eventually experience whatever you need to fully maximize your growth potential. Call it punishment if you must."

"And the punishment can happen lifetimes later?"

"Yes. Karma is like a mischievous child. You never know when it will jump out from behind a tree. But you must not fear karma. It always works for your ultimate good. Even your present pain over James will be for your enlightenment. God has willed it. Yours is a love for the ages."

"What can I do to set things right?"

"I think there is much we can do if you are truly willing to sacrifice yourself. I can suggest several healing rituals, using crystals, flowers, and intense meditation. And you must also pray that you and James will finally consummate your forever love."

Had Sara stepped back and seriously considered what she was about to do, even she might have said she was totally out of her mind. But she was broken and vulnerable, susceptible to anything that offered any hope of resolving the conflicts in her life. Karma and reincarnation were new concepts to her, but they were sufficiently intriguing that she was willing to give them an audience—particularly if they could really perform as advertised.

Any thoughts of non-Christian heresy were quickly dismissed. Had she not felt from the very beginning that she had somehow known James before? What else could explain that feeling unless Tina was right? "Maybe," thought Sara, "just maybe what the Bible tells us is truth, but not the whole truth." And with that musing, Sara gave up any remaining doubts.

3

◆

Romancing
the Crystal

The healing ritual was designed to purify the chakras, or seven healing areas of the body. For that, Tina needed seven large amethysts. Amethysts are a purple-to-violet variety of quartz thought to have curative powers for various kinds of karmic distress. "The ancient Greeks," said Tina, "understood that this particular crystal could prevent intoxication, and so they named it *amethyst*. It comes from *methystos*, meaning 'drunken,' and *a*, meaning 'not.' Not drunken."

"I don't have a drinking problem," Sara said with a smile.

"Sure you do," Tina quickly rejoined. "You're intoxicated with unrequited love."

Sara laughed. "But how is a rock supposed to heal the pain and hurt of unrequited love?"

"It's a matter of energy. Our souls are made up of energy. When there is psychic stress, the energy is dissipated. Do you remember crystal radios?"

"I'm afraid they were a bit before my time."

"Mine, too, really. But they operated on the same principle. Radio waves—energy—were conducted by crystals. Crystals concentrate energy where it is needed. What you need is like an energy fill-up to replenish what the strain of this relationship has taken out of you. The source of this energy is what Christians refer to as the Holy Spirit. The Holy Spirit is simply ultimate energy, or God Force. It is not the crystal itself, but God Force that is going to heal you."

"Is it the same as what the Bible refers to as the *power* of God?"

"Exactly. God Force is energy, and energy is power."

Sara wasn't sure about this metaphysical explanation, especially when it came to redefining the Holy Spirit as energy, and God as "God Force." But still she was committed to the healing process. So committed, in fact, that when Tina said the seven crystals would cost 120 dollars, Sara hardly blinked. She had seen cheap crystals for sale in smartly merchandised packages at popular bookstores, right next to the New Age section, but she had always thought of them as trendy gimmicks. Her need of healing was real, and well worth whatever it might cost.

Tina assured Sara that she would never suggest a ritual that wasn't absolutely necessary. When Sara mentioned that she was living month to month with very little savings, Tina told her to pay what she could afford and she would loan her the rest. She could pay Tina back as she had the money.

Whenever more money was needed for future rituals (and there would be much more money to come), Sara always considered it an important spiritual sacrifice that she needed to make in order to cleanse her karma. She also figured that she needed to prove she wasn't a slave to money or worldly things. For Sara, the money paid to a psychic took on the same meaning as tithing in the church.

Sara handed over what money she had in her purse, 70 dollars, and Tina told her to come back the following Monday. In the meantime Tina would purchase the amethysts.

—— ◆ ——

Tina had turned down the lights in the room and focused a spotlight on the seven amethysts, now placed in a row left to right from smallest to largest, on a narrow table which reminded Sara of the communion table at her church. The thought quickly crossed her mind that the scene was reminiscent of a religious altar.

Tina directed Sara to the center of the room, where there was a tubular metal pyramid.

"What is this for?" Sara inquired.

"Have you ever heard of 'pyramid power'? Like the crystals, the shape of the pyramid also has the ability to focus energy. That's why the ancient Egyptians buried their pharaohs beneath the great pyramids in anticipation of their afterlives.

"If you want to see something interesting, the next time you have a dollar bill in your hand look on the back side of Washington's picture and you'll see a pyramid, with the top part of it enveloping 'the third eye.' The Founding Fathers were not so much Christians as they were spiritualists. They understood both pyramid power and the metaphysical enlightenment which 'the third eye' represents.

"At the beginning of our country, we trusted in God Force because of the great energy level which came from the influx of highly evolved spiritual beings who were arriving, not just from England, but also from the lost continent of Atlantis. Whether in Egypt, or Atlantis, or in the early days of the United States, pyramid power has played an important role in helping us focus on the energy of God Force."

With the history lesson over, Tina invited Sara to sit in the center of the pyramid in the lotus position and to meditate. Although she sensed no sudden surge of energy, Sara felt comfortable and at ease within herself. As she concentrated on the deep purple amethysts on the table before her, she was certain that psychic healing was taking place. All she could think about was getting rid of her bad karma so she could once again be united in love with her soul mate, James. As Tina had said, surely it was a "love for the ages"!

—— ◆ ——

The water in the bath rippled quietly around Sara's body as she gently moved her hands back and forth in a sculling motion. The ritual bath was to be another way of getting in touch with God Force, which the surrounding water represented. As Tina had instructed her, Sara tried to imagine an aura of white light also surrounding her body. Again as instructed, Sara slowly removed one petal after another from a red rose which she had bought that afternoon. She let the petals float around her. They symbolized the forever love which she and James shared.

After praying and meditating (mostly praying, since that was a form more familiar to her), Sara got out of the tub and collected the petals from the water. She was to take them to Tina the next day. Sara was amazed that the petals had not wilted, even in the warm bathwater. They were in perfect condition!

When Tina examined the petals the next afternoon, she confirmed James' love for Sara. Their love was true and was definitely God's will. But, of course, the more confirmation the better. Other rituals would be necessary.

If someone had suggested she was getting involved in witchcraft through these rituals, Sara would have been shocked. There was no hint of secret potions, child sacrifice, seances with the dead, or any of the other things one would normally associate with witchcraft. It would never have occurred to Sara that she was playing in the devil's workshop. None of his normal tools were lying about. Tina herself never once mentioned Satan— only God.

No, Sara was completely at ease with the rituals. They were God's way of bringing about spiritual healing in her life. Why else would Tina ask Sara to spend three nights in *prayer* for James?

—— ◆ ——

On the first night Sara waited until dark, then lay on her bed imagining an orange light surrounding her body. Tina had said that she had three chakras that needed continual healing: one orange, one yellow, and one purple. These chakras mainly had to do with affairs of the heart. Tina had given Sara a white candle with an angel on it. Sara was to light the candle during the prayer-and-meditation ceremony on each of the three nights.

After concentrating on the candle's flame for half an hour, Sara meditated about James, sending him her positive thoughts and love. After that she prayed a prayer that Tina had given her to conclude the ritual with each night: "Dear Lord, free the one I love from all negative beings. Free both of us and guide us into the light. Show us the light. Amen."

Tina had explained the importance of light in psychic healing. It really meant en*light*enment, the triumph of truth over metaphysical ignorance. She had said that this was what Jesus meant when he said, "I am the light of the world." Wasn't Jesus the most enlightened being who had ever existed? When God first said, "Let there be light," what he meant was, "Let there be enlightenment." Hence the significance of the candle and its light.

On the second night Sara imagined her body being surrounded by both a yellow and an orange light. On the third night it was all three: orange, yellow, and purple. Whatever the color, night after night Sara earnestly sought God's will in the flickering flame.

— ◆ —

The bedsheets had the luxurious feel of soft pima cotton and the distinctive just-off-the-shelf smell of new linens. Putting 200 dollars on her VISA card, Sara had purchased Sears' finest bedding: a comforter, pillowcases, twin sheets (representing the two children she and James were to have), and towels. The towels were orange, yellow, and purple, in keeping with the chakras to be healed. Tina had stressed that all the bedding was to be in bright healing colors. (Light manifests itself in a rainbow of colors, Tina had explained. Chakras, colors, light, and enlightenment are all psychically interrelated.)

As she snuggled between the sheets, Sara thought back on the strange odyssey that had begun when she first walked through Tina's door. She was amazed at how her initial skepticism had all but vanished. In the ensuing weeks of seeing Tina, Sara had felt more and more at peace. She felt free and in control of her destiny. Her whole life seemed on track.

Bob was completely out of her life now, and she felt no sense of loss. Her body felt as light as a feather. People around her would often comment on how "glowing" she looked. Men were drawn to her more than ever. She had even begun to trust men again. And that was important to this particular ritual.

The bed linen was supposed to represent James' sexual attraction for her. Tina had been upset to learn that Sara had not had sex with James. "Having sex would have established an irreversible connection to James. It would have made our work so much easier!"

So there she was, lying between brightly colored, soft-as-satin sheets feeling remorse that she was still a virgin. "Did James and I ever make love with each other in our previous lives?" Sara mused dreamily. "Surely Tina was right. Why did I send him away the night he wanted to sleep over? What could be more right than making love with my soul mate?"

And with that thought, Sara closed her eyes and fell asleep.

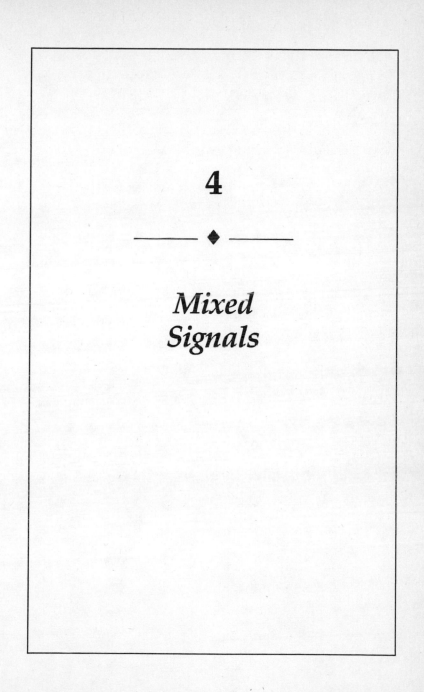

4

Mixed Signals

Throughout the weeks that Sara had been under Tina's spiritual guidance, Sara was hesitant to mention her psychic experience to her Christian friends. Afraid that they would not have a positive reaction to it, she avoided any mention of it. Sara was operating on two different levels: Sara the Christian and Sara the psychic searcher. Deep down, on one level, she knew the truth: She shouldn't be messing around with psychic powers and pagan rituals. But on a more immediate level, Sara felt that Tina's psychic ability was a real power helping her. Knowing who she was going to marry and spend the rest of her life with gave Sara inner peace like she had never before experienced.

That assurance had given Sara a new sense of direction. It was the kind of guidance that she had never gotten from her church. Where organized religion was mostly interested in questions of sin and salvation, what Sara felt she needed at the present moment was answers to questions about her personal life. Who at church would have dared to help identify her soul mate? She had turned to Tina for that kind of information, and Tina had given her "the truth." Even so, Sara was certain that this was not something her Christian friends would understand or accept as real.

In the process of seeking psychic answers, Sara never lost her faith in God. In fact, she never stopped going to church on Sunday. But as she sat in the pew and went through the motions of familiar worship, she was less of a participant and more of an observer. Traditional worship ritual was less personal than was psychic ritual. In fact, Sara thought, what they were doing in worship was more *ritual* than *spiritual*. The two rarely seemed to connect. What relevance did even the ritual have in her life? Why did she feel so little moved in her inner self?

Sara's church was what some might call a "high church," with lots of pomp and circumstance. All the right ecclesiastical words were said, but she had never been able to pierce through the ceremony to touch God. For that she had relied on her own prayers. Nor did she really know the Bible. The sermons frequently focused on social and political issues. There was poetry and interesting anecdotes, but little reference to the Scriptures. Sara had always felt somewhat handicapped because of her ignorance of the Scriptures. At college, many of Sara's Christian classmates could quote book, chapter, and verse at the drop of a hat. How Sara envied them!

Sometimes while she was sitting in church, Sara would be listening only halfheartedly to the drone of a sanctimonious sermon, and she would let her mind wander. On one occasion she questioned whether the majority of Christians were right in thinking that Christianity and psychics were mutually exclusive. From what she had experienced, it was like God was telling her the truth through Tina, and that Tina was simply God's instrument for good. Sara never felt like Tina was from the devil. How could such a feeling of spiritual fulfillment *not* be from God?

Apart from her strong belief in God, Sara began to question almost everything else she had always believed. "Maybe we don't have the *ability* to be certain about everything," she thought. "After all, we're only human."

In particular, Sara tinkered with the thought that maybe reincarnation was for real—that maybe we come back until we get right with God and *then* he takes us to heaven. She was pretty sure this was contrary to Scripture, and yet somehow she couldn't help entertaining the thought that it could be true.

Sara herself recognized the irony. The more she thought she understood about herself and her future, the more uncertainty she faced. As far as her faith was concerned, everything but God's love had become unclear. The tension between her Christian faith and her new trust in psychic power had cast doubt on everything. More than anything during this period, she experienced the inability to distinguish truth from lies. She couldn't tell what was from the enemy and what was from God. She had lost all discernment.

At one point during her psychic experience, Sara went to the beach to pray and meditate. She was overcome with an indescribable spiritual "Presence" and a special feeling of peace. To her great delight, what she saw was a vision of herself and James with "their children." Surely it was a vision from God! But almost immediately she sensed another "presence"—some enemy trying to keep James and her apart. What was she to make of it all? Where could she turn? Who could she trust?

— ◆ —

As if her growing spiritual conflicts were not enough, things were not going well at her new job. Sara had worked only two weeks at the clothing boutique when her boss, a married man with three children, started sexually harassing her in the employee lounge. Whenever they were alone, he was all over her. Although Sara had done nothing to encourage his aggression, she nevertheless felt dirty and cheap.

And that was only a prelude to what turned out to be far more disastrous. At a party which she knew she should never have gone to in the first place, two creeps in respectable-looking suits and ties slipped a hallucinatory drug into her drink, then took her to a bedroom where they sexually assaulted her. She just thanked God that they had left her a virgin— barely.

Naturally, her trust of men, which had always been a struggle for her, hit rock bottom. Under the circumstances, Tina's continual, warm, reassuring affirmations couldn't have been more timely. Sara hungered for love and protection. Hers was an ongoing battle of heart and mind. She couldn't tell who were the devils and who were the angels. But for now, Tina was her guardian angel.

Or was she? Even that thought was not always comforting. No other "guardian angel" had ever cost her so much. It wasn't long before a lot of money had been exchanged between Sara and Tina. The rituals were never cheap. And in addition to the money, Sara sometimes took groceries for Tina's baby. For awhile, the mounting cost of Tina's services seemed to Sara a necessary sacrifice. But one thing after another started to bother Sara.

During one of her visits to Tina, Tina said that it would be best if payment for the next ritual could be made by the end of the month—that the healing process would be better before that time! The obvious self-serving convenience of the payment was not lost on Sara.

On another occasion Tina wanted Sara to buy a set of amethysts for James, just as she had done for herself. James too needed healing, Tina had said. Of course, that meant another 120 dollars for seven more large crystals. That too smacked of commercialism.

Most of all, however, Sara wasn't quite sure about the 100 dollars' worth of Crown Royal whiskey that Tina insisted she buy. (Even then, Sara wondered whether that might not be for Tina's husband more than for her healing!) Supposedly the four large bottles of Canadian whiskey were necessary for warding off any thoughts that James might have of being tempted back to Diana.

Naturally, Sara considered the possibility that Tina was just ripping her off; but to her own amazement, she dismissed these strange financial arrangements as mere psychic eccentricity. It was the results that counted, and in that ballpark Tina was still hitting home runs.

When Sara and Tina got together, Tina would give a kind of progress report. She would tell Sara what her meditations had revealed. Perhaps it would be about James and Diana and how they were getting along. Their relationship was always up and down, but for the most part the news was usually encouraging. There was the time, however, when Tina was discouraged because James wasn't fighting hard enough to be with Sara. He was slipping back into Diana's clutches. So it wasn't always good news, but Tina never gave up hope.

"Who else has given me hope lately?" Sara asked herself. And so the weeks with Tina turned into months.

—— ◆ ——

Discernment. Sara reached the point where what she wanted most was *discernment*. She had become spiritually schizophrenic. By now her room was filled with books which Tina had encouraged her to read. There was Marilyn Ferguson's *Aquarian Conspiracy*, which Tina had called "the handbook of the New Age movement." It had opened Sara's eyes to the unbelievably broad networking of New Age thought and practice since the sixties. Psychic power and spiritual healing were only part of a wide-ranging eclectic belief system that was sweeping the country. New Age thinking was ushering in a new age of metaphysical enlightenment.

Then there was the voluminous (and expensive) *Course in Miracles* which had been recommended by a New Age enthusiast that Sara had met at the Bodhi Tree bookstore. The Bodhi Tree was a kind of mecca for psychics and New Agers looking for books on meditation, astral projection, karma, Shiatsu massage, holistic medicine, and virtually anything else one might desire in the cosmic arena of esoterica.

Sara had spent long nights working her way through the Course's process of "removing the blocks to the awareness of love's presence." The Course used familiar Christian terminology, like *sin* and *forgiveness*, but Sara was troubled when it said that sin is only an illusion—a dream from which we must awaken.

"Could that really be from God?" Sara asked herself, knowing in her heart that it wasn't. Nor was Sara sure about the Course's psychological redefinition of *miracle* as "a divine intervention in our minds which heals our thought-patterns." Is that really what Jesus did when he walked on water and fed the five thousand?

Other books had introduced Sara to unfamiliar Eastern religions like Hinduism, Buddhism, Confucianism, Taoism—even ancient Zoroastrianism. Tina had talked about all of these religions as containing expressions of God's love. "Look around you, Sara," Tina had said. "There is good in all religions. And because God is good, it means that there is *God* in all religions."

By comparison with her struggling attempts to comprehend major world religions, it took only a few hours to skim through each of Shirley MacLaine's popular bio-novels in which she chronicles her spiritual wanderings from the beach at Malibu to Machu Picchu, home of the ancient Incas of Peru.

Tina was enamored with Shirley MacLaine, though she acknowledged that most of her fellow psychics considered Shirley's brand of New Age thinking to be mostly commercialized fluff. Tina, who didn't mind poking fun at her own profession, once laughed about her favorite cartoon, of the man in the cemetery who suddenly realizes that every tombstone has Shirley MacLaine's name engraved on it—each with different dates down through history!

Whatever her credentials among more intellectual New Agers, it was Shirley MacLaine who had introduced Sara to the father of modern psychic thought, the late Edgar Cayce. By now Sara had consumed several books published by Cayce's Association for Research and Enlightenment out of Virginia Beach. Sara found Cayce absolutely fascinating, and in a way, a mirror of her own spiritual schizophrenia. Cayce had been a Sunday school teacher before becoming well-known for psychic healing and reincarnational revelations. Somehow Cayce was able to reconcile his belief in the Bible with his belief in psychic phenomena.

Sara was impressed at Cayce's seemingly near-perfect record in psychically diagnosing physical illnesses and prescribing appropriate treatments even though he had had no medical training whatsoever. It made Sara trust all the more Cayce's claims to know about people's past lives. If he had the power to bring about psychic healing, then maybe there was something to reincarnation after all. And if reincarnation was for real, then surely Tina was right about Sara's connection with James in a previous lifetime!

It was all terribly intriguing. But Sara had to admit that reincarnation and Buddhism and out-of-body experiences were a lot to swallow—especially when almost every strand of New Age thought and practice was mixed in with Christianity. It wasn't anything like the Christianity she had always known.

After one particular late night of troublesome reading, Sara's house of cards came tumbling down. "What am I supposed to believe?" Sara sobbed into her pillow. "I don't know anything anymore. I just don't know. I just don't know."

There would be no sleeping that night.

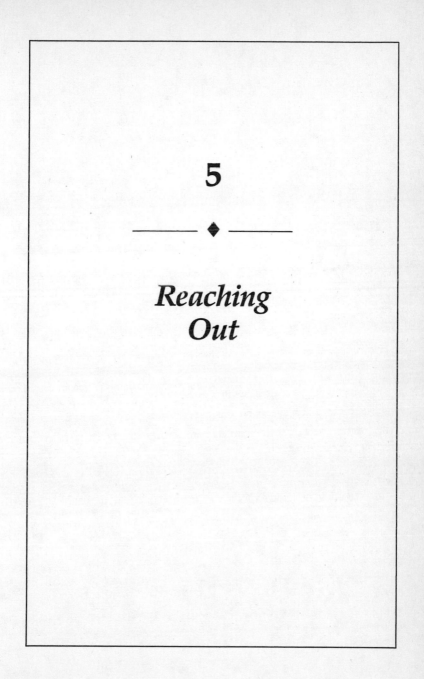

5

Reaching Out

Eric? I'm hoping that you remember me. I'm Sara from the English Lit class. I sat a few seats to your left. You were a senior when I was a sophomore, so you might not have taken any notice."

"Oh, yeah. Jet black hair, long. Wicked sense of humor?"

"Did I *ever* have a sense of humor? It must have been ages ago. But, yep, that's me. What are you doing these days?"

"Believe it or not, I'm a second-year law student at the University. Right now for the summer I'm clerking in a big firm downtown. Puttin' in those billable hours every day as if I were a high-priced lawyer!"

"Hey, that's great. Let me know when you become that rich lawyer!" Sara laughed nervously, then hesitated. "Listen, I hope I'm not bothering you, but your name popped into my mind last night. I was just wondering . . . are you still involved in Christian activities?" Sara's face was almost grimacing as she asked the question.

"Sure am. Don't know how I could survive without the Bible studies and fellowship. They're my lifeline."

Sara relaxed again. "It's funny. I remember the time you challenged Dr. Bernstein when she shocked us with that radical pro-choice lecture that came right out of the blue. You were great! She didn't know what had hit her!"

"Yeah, that was quite a session, wasn't it? I couldn't believe my ears when she said she even favored infanticide where the baby was born handicapped. What was it she called it—a 30-day return policy? Man!

"The absolutely weirdest part, remember, was when she said that aborted fetuses were disembodied spiritual entities who had decided to come to the planet from the astral plane, but for some reason had a change of mind and decided to 'check out.' Do you remember what she said when I asked her whether the fetus caused its own abortion?"

"Oh, yeah," Sara picked up with a burst of memory that came flashing out of the past. "Something like, 'The fetus communicates psychically with the mother, telling her to have an abortion.'"

"Exactly! Was that incredible or what! I wonder what in the world she was into?"

Sara paused, wondering whether perhaps she had made a mistake in calling Eric. But she took a deep breath and said, "Eric, I think I know what she was into, and that's why I'm calling. I don't really know how to put this, but . . . well, I think I'm into some of the same stuff."

"Really?"

"Not the psychic abortions and infanticide bit, but . . . well . . . just psychic stuff in general. I've been toying with it for several months now, seeing a psychic and doing a lot of reading about reincarnation and Eastern mysticism. It's all very confusing."

"But I thought you were a Christian. Didn't you come to one of our Bible studies that year?"

"Yeah, and that's why I decided to call you. I still remember how well you knew the Bible, and how ignorant I felt by comparison. I *am* a Christian, but I've sorta let my faith get away from me lately. At the very least, I'm confused about what I believe these days. Eric, I really need to talk to someone. Could you possibly meet me sometime?"

"Sure. I'll be happy to do whatever I can. When do you want to get together?"

———— ◆ ————

Sara sat nervously waiting for Eric to arrive. He had suggested that, since it was the Fourth of July, he wasn't clerking and had nothing to do until later in the afternoon, when he was supposed to go to a cookout at his sister's. Why didn't they meet right away at the Big Boy located midway between where each of them lived? he had suggested. Sara was greatly relieved that Eric had agreed to meet her, and that she didn't have to wait another day. Even a day later and she was afraid she might have backed out.

The little American flag sticking out of the artificial flower arrangement on the table reminded Sara that it was in fact Independence Day. The irony didn't escape her. She was feeling *anything* but *free* these days. And she couldn't believe she was so caught up in her spiritual struggle that she had forgotten it was the Fourth of July.

That thought lingered. Sara began thinking how engrossed in herself she had been for the whole of these many weeks. All she had thought about was herself. Her pain, her confusion, her feelings, her future—even her faith had become self-centered. It had been ages since she had spent time with her folks, or done anything to help anyone else. In her spiritual search she had managed to isolate herself from everything and everyone—just taking, never giving.

It occurred to her that there might be some parallels between her growing interest in New Age philosophy and the increasing distance she felt from her Christian roots. As she thought about it, Jesus' teaching was always meant to nudge a person out of self and into the love and service of others. In her heart she knew that Jesus was pointing the way to true happiness. By contrast, Sara had to admit that New Age literature centered almost entirely on the self—higher self, lower self, self-awareness, self-empowerment, self-exploration, and on and on. Sara wondered, "If we are what we *eat*, do we also become what we *read*?"

"Sara?" It was Eric, right on the dot.

"Hi. Thanks for coming. It's been such a long time, I didn't know whether you would remember. We never got to know each other very well, did we?"

"No, but weren't you the one who busted the curve on the final exam?"

"Guilty, your honor."

"Can I take your order?" interrupted the waitress.

"Listen, it won't be long before I'm having a hamburger. I think I'll just have a glass of iced tea."

"Me too," said Sara. She was too nervous to eat in any event.

"Eric, I guess you must think I'm out of my head, and sometimes I wonder myself, but I really didn't have anyone else to talk to. I suppose you're my 'Greyhound bus syndrome.'"

"Greyhound bus syndrome?"

"Yeah. You know how when you're on a bus or a plane and tell things to complete strangers that you would never tell to your best friends? It's because it's safe. After all, who are they going to tell?"

"I guess you're right," Eric said with an appreciative smile. "No wonder you were a curve buster!"

"I've been wanting to talk to someone for several weeks now, but I just couldn't tell any of my friends at church—A, because they wouldn't understand, and B, because it wouldn't be long before everyone in the church had heard the rumor that I was into witchcraft. Christians are as good at gossip as anyone else."

"Would you believe *better*?" he asked.

"So, here I am, ready to pour out my heart and soul."

"Pour on, Macduff."

Sara took a sip of her iced tea and began telling her story. All the bits—the good, the bad, even the embarrassing. With each statement she carefully read Eric's reaction, and with each statement she felt more and more at ease. Eric was listening intently, warmly, and nonjudgmentally. Whenever she raced ahead too fast, Eric asked just the right question to help her fill in the gaps.

"Bodhi Tree? Wasn't that the tree that Buddha used to sit under or something?"

"Yeah. There's a lot of Buddhism in New Age literature. Jesus is quoted more often, but Buddha is everyone's secret hero. I suspect it's because Buddha talks only about good things, whereas Jesus ends up talking about hell!"

"It's probably the same reason why reincarnation is so appealing. No one has to come to grips with the reality of eternal judgment."

It was a comfortable give-and-take. Sara knew she was talking to a friend she could trust. More than that, here was a brother in Christ listening to a sister in Christ whom he respected. Sara knew that he was empathetic with all the hurt and pain that she had experienced.

"And that's when I decided to call you. I was tossing and turning in total confusion, not knowing whether I was a Christian, a New Ager, or both. I just didn't know who or what to trust anymore. Frankly, I'm just spiritually drained!"

"It's quite a story all right," Eric said as he leaned back in the booth. I'm not exactly sure how you want me to respond. There's a lot you've told me that I've never heard about before, so it's somewhat difficult to react to it. On the other hand, the good news is that we're just now beginning a special class at our church on the New Age movement. So maybe I can catch up quickly.

"Now there's an idea. Would you like to come to the class with me?"

Sara hesitated. She wasn't sure she was ready for a full frontal assault. "I don't know, Eric. It may be too soon for me. I was hoping I could just use you as a sounding board and work through some of this for myself. Would you be willing to do that for me?"

"Absolutely. No problem. It will motivate me to read some of the material that's going to be covered in the class. In fact, it will also help me talk more knowledgeably with one of the partners at the law firm. He told me the other day that he and his wife are developing an interest in the New Age movement. I instantly felt out of my depth.

"Do you still have some of your books from the Bodhi Tree?"

"Sure. You're welcome to borrow them. But I'm warning you, it's pretty mind-blowing stuff."

"Well, it couldn't be much more mind-blowing than some of the ACLU-supported gay rights and pornography cases we have to read in my Law and Morality seminar. Besides," Eric chuckled, "all that right-brain intuitive stuff will give the left side of my brain a rest!"

Sara thought to herself, "Thank you, Lord. You've brought the right person into my life. No one at my church would have the foggiest idea about all that trendy right brain/left brain psychobabble."

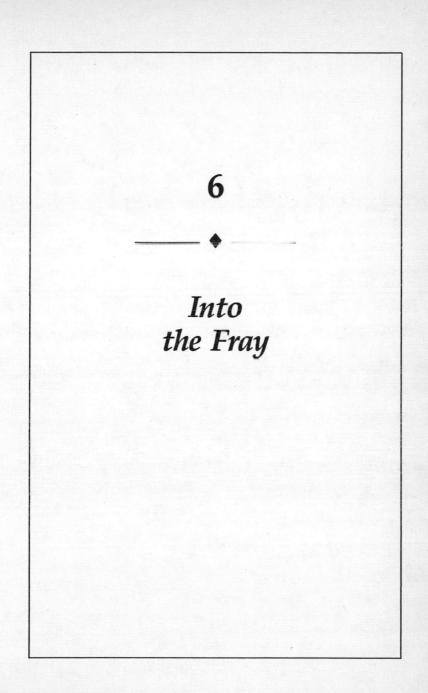

6

Into
the Fray

Eric showed up carrying a stack of a dozen books under his arm. "Doing some light reading, are we?" Sara teased.

"Some of it is light, all right. So light it practically floats away into the astral plane. But some of it is also—what was your word—*mind-boggling*? Take, for instance, all that hypnotic regression stuff in this book here." Eric pointed to Helen Wambach's book *Life Before Life.*

"Surely you aren't doubting that people can be regressed hypnotically in order to remember things they've forgotten about in their past. Don't they do that even in court these days, to refresh the witness' recollection?"

"Sure, but what they remember is within their own lifetime, within a verifiable context—not something from past lives hundreds of years ago when they claim to be, who knows, the Sultan of Arabia. And if the regressions had taken place in a trial, I would have objected to all the leading questions. There seemed to be an incredibly high suggestibility factor.

"What I found most interesting was the kind of people who were undergoing the regression. Wambach herself admitted that virtually all of them already believed that they had lived past lives and were anxious to learn the details. Wasn't it 81 percent of her subjects who said that they themselves had chosen to be born? They were not exactly what I would have called disinterested witnesses. Is it memory or just someone's vivid imagination?"

Sara laughed. "Did I make a big mistake asking a soon-to-be-lawyer to be my sounding board?"

"Maybe so," Eric grinned, "but think of the good side: You get me before I've passed the bar, so you don't have to pay through the nose for all this high-powered advice!

"By the way, did you spot what I did when you were reading the book? Dr. Bernstein must have been reading Wambach! Look, right here on page 121 is that bit about psychic abortion. And if that weren't sufficiently outrageous, look at the next sentence: 'Perhaps the sudden death syndrome in infants may be the result of a soul's decision not to go ahead with a life plan.' Incredible!

"I tell you, Sara, for my money New Age cynicism about the value of human life is itself enough for me to reject it."

"I agree that some of the New Age authors seem to go overboard at times, and I have to admit that it bothers me. But the same thing could be said about a lot of Christians. Have you seen all the Christian crazies running around out there?"

"Yeah, I know, but if New Agers are going to claim that everyone has lived scores or even hundreds of past lives, there's got to be better proof of it than something as manipulatable as hypnotic regression."

"How about déjà vu? Don't you ever experience those times when you just *know* you've lived that same experience before? That's what first led me into thinking that reincarnation might be for real. Honestly, when James and I had that first dinner together, I knew I had known him before—like for a lifetime. It was as if we had been sitting there in that same restaurant before, ordering off the same menu, eating the same food. So when Tina said that her meditations revealed that we in fact *had* been together in a previous lifetime, it all made sense. I still have to believe it. The feeling I had was too strong to deny."

"I've experienced déjà vu myself, lots of times. But isn't that the whole point? When you experience déjà vu you think you have already seen *exactly* what you are seeing at that very moment. So if it's a restaurant you're in, it will look exactly like a restaurant in this lifetime, not some restaurant a hundred or a thousand years ago. The same goes for the menus, and what you're wearing, and the car you drove to the restaurant in. No one seems to know for sure what causes déjà vu, but it certainly can't be offered as proof of past lives. By definition, déjà vu always implies that 'the past' is exactly the same as whatever is happening in the *present* moment."

"So what do *you* think explains déjà vu?" asked Sara, putting Eric on the defensive.

"If you want my best guess, I suspect that what takes place in déjà vu is not terribly unlike what happens when a television picture breaks up and you see some actor on the screen in a series of stop-action freeze frames. Like televisions, our minds also transmit images electronically. So if there were to be a breakup in transmission, it's possible that we could experience a similar stop-action, freeze-frame phenomenon. If we think we've seen something before, we *have*. Not in some past life, but only milliseconds before when the image first hit our brain!"

Eric knew he was out of his field. "How's that for jumping in where angels fear to tread?" he said with a broad smile.

"I don't know, but I have this overwhelming feeling that I've heard it somewhere before, and that you were wearing the exact same shirt!" Sara exclaimed with a wicked little smirk. Eric let out a hearty laugh.

"Technically speaking, you're probably right that déjà vu itself has some physiological explanation," Sara conceded, "but what I felt that first night with James was nothing physiological. It was not so much in my mind as in my soul."

"Listen, Sara, one of the things I like about you is your basic honesty. So tell me if you can: Do you think you ever would have even considered reincarnation to be possible if you weren't so intent on verifying your feelings for James? I know it's a tough question, but what do you think?"

Sara thought for a moment. "Honestly? I'd have to say that probably . . . probably I would never have entertained reincarnation as a possibility. I remember when Tina first confirmed that James was my soul mate. At the moment she said we had been together in a previous life, I'm sure I must have flinched. Frankly, I had never before thought about reincarnation one way or the other. All I knew was that it was a widely held belief in some religions."

"I've got a hunch that reincarnation appeals to a lot of people because it provides a simple explanation for the inexplicable. From what I read in some of your books, that's how reincarnation got started in the first place. People in the midst of suffering, especially people in the Indian subcontinent where life was miserable, asked what we all ask about pain and suffering: What did I do to deserve this? That's what karma is all about—cause and effect.

"But then someone looked at a child who was born with a physical disability, and the obvious question was, If the disability is an *effect*, when could there have been a *cause* unless it happened in some previous lifetime? And because it was a *simple* explanation, it hardly seemed to matter whether or not it was the *right* explanation."

"Assuming you're right," Sara extended the logic, "I suppose it would be especially true if the one who was asking the question just happened to have been the child's parent. He or she would have *wanted* to believe there was an explanation—*any* explanation."

"In your case," Eric continued, "there you are, desperately looking for answers to your love life, and Tina comes along and tells you something that, although it's highly improbable, you're willing to buy for lack of a better alternative.

"No offense, but I wonder if in your particular case you weren't vulnerable to the idea of reincarnation because you so desperately wanted to believe that James was your soul mate?"

"You may be right," Sara conceded, "but might we not believe in heaven for all the same reasons? Just because we *want* to believe that there is a heaven when we die doesn't make it any more certain to exist than reincarnation."

Eric smiled. "Right, but then that leaves us needing more objective proof of either one or the other afterlife explanations, not just our desire or hope that one of them might be true. Which brings me back to India. Now there's what I call a good lab project for testing the theory of reincarnation. There's a culture that has believed in reincarnation for several thousand years. If they are right about spiritual evolution working through centuries of reincarnation, then why is their society still bogged down in such abysmal misery and hopelessness? I went there last summer, and you wouldn't believe the appalling conditions. Worse yet, no one there seems to care!"

"Aren't you focusing on economic conditions rather than spiritual values? Who's to say that we materialistic Americans are any less impoverished in soul?"

"Good point. And yet you have to admit that it's only been Christian relief agencies that have made any serious effort to help the underclass in India. Because of the pervasive belief in karma and its resulting caste system, there's no incentive for the Brahmins at the top of the social ladder to help the 'untouchables' down there at the bottom. In fact, there is every reason *not* to provide assistance. Helping them may well get in the way of their working out their bad karma.

"No way!" Eric affirmed, as if to himself. "I can't believe that the end product of centuries of spiritual enlightenment would be an acceptable attitude that simply ignores the suffering."

Sara managed a smile. "You're tough, counselor, awfully tough!"

"So are you, my friend. I'm just glad I'm not having to worry about you busting curves on my law school exams!"

Eric was silent for a minute, then looked up again. "If I were to play devil's advocate, I'd have to ask about what looks for all intents and purposes to be some kind of spiritual evolution in the Bible. When you look back in the Old Testament at the earliest centuries of mankind's existence, you see a pretty brutal culture, even among the children of Israel. There's all that stoning people for offenses against the laws of Moses, and the brutality of killing men, women, and children in battle. By New Testament times, you begin to see a more civilized society . . . well, somewhat, at least. Then compare that to our culture at the end of the twentieth century. We've come a long way, haven't we? Could that be evidence of spiritual progress?"

Sara countered: "Well, if *I* were playing devil's advocate, I'd have to point out the many atrocities in our own century, and the fact that human nature never seems to change.

"Which Bible character was it that said, 'There is nothing new under the sun'?"

"Solomon."

"Yeah. On the other hand, I also suspect that Jesus' teaching probably catapulted mankind into a higher spiritual order than was ever the case under Jewish law alone. I get the feeling that Christianity brought about a moral quantum leap.

"Maybe you're already rubbing off on me," Sara confessed, "but I also have to admit that I get bothered when child prodigies are offered up as proof of past lives. Did you run across that in your reading?"

"You mean, something about the accumulated talent of many past lives manifesting itself in the four-year-old whiz kid?"

"Yeah," said Sara. "But not even I buy that. Child prodigies still have to learn how to eat and be potty-trained. If talent is accumulated, why not knowledge as well?"

"Wow!" Eric exclaimed. "You don't need me anymore. You're doing great all by yourself!"

"I don't know. Neither side seems to be airtight. We don't have an awful lot of folks coming back from heaven or hell to confirm that route either."

Eric had a thought. "But didn't you just hit on something with the child prodigy example? If in fact we've had prior lives, wouldn't we remember them? In technicolor?"

Sara was ready for this one. "You know the answer New Agers give to that, of course. There is supposed to be what they call a 'veil of forgetfulness' that prevents that from happening—perhaps so that we aren't so traumatized by our misspent past that we are prevented from learning the lessons we need to learn in this life. Besides, can you remember what happened to you even when you were two days old?"

"Ummm . . . no!" Eric floundered for the first time. "Just because you can't *remember* doesn't mean you didn't *exist,* does it?" Sara sensed she had won an important battle.

Eric paused. "Let me think about this for a minute. Oh, here we go. The problem is still there. What good does it do us to have lived past lives if we can't remember the lessons we were supposed to have learned?"

Sara was less certain about her response this time. "I'm not sure I understand or buy this answer, but wasn't it Shirley MacLaine in one of her books who said we have two different selves—our higher selves and our lower selves, and that even if our lower self doesn't remember, our higher self does?"

"Oh, yeah, I remember that part. But even when I read it I thought what a convenient, self-serving, nonexplanation it was. If we are cosmically schizophrenic, how are we ever supposed to get our act together? Do our higher selves and our lower selves ever talk to each other? And if so—if our higher selves have already benefited from the accumulated wisdom of the ages, then why the charade of the lower self having to keep reincarnating lifetime after lifetime?

"Oh, and I almost forgot the other problem I was thinking about the other day." Eric rushed on. "Just suppose there is such a thing as karma, and that when you do something bad you get assigned to some lower level of existence. How do you ever get out of the downward tailspin? No one is perfect. We all have bad karma, if you want to put it that way. So how could anyone ever evolve spiritually?

"Wouldn't it be like a pilot of a light plane that goes into a sudden dive? The more the plane lurches forward, the more the pilot's body is thrown against the stick. The more his body is thrown against the stick, the more the plane lurches forward, and so on till it crashes. If you leave the grace of God out of the equation, none of us will ever make it. There's just no way we can bootstrap ourselves into perfection."

Sara knew that was a good answer. She wished Tina could be there to join in the conversation. On second thought, Sara was pretty sure Tina would be out of her depth with all this intellectual analysis. Tina was more a hands-on person than a New Age scholar, if there were such a person.

"You've given me lots to think about, Eric. I'm going to have to run for now, but I'd like to meet again next Friday, if that's still good for you."

"It's perfect."

"I guess I should say, 'Almost thou persuadest me.' But I'll tell you what still bothers me. It's Edgar Cayce's life readings. They're amazing. Simply amazing. And he was a Christian! If I identify with anyone in the New Age movement, it's Cayce. Can we talk about him next time?"

Eric had the look of a fox that had just captured his prey. "Cayce next time? You bet. I can't wait!"

"Don't look so smug," Sara said as she planted a kiss on Eric's cheek and dashed toward her car.

7

◆

Psychic
Faux Pas

When he arrived, Eric was mumbling something about the pressure of putting in enough hours at the firm, and about how little sleep he was getting these days. But he was raring to get on with their discussion of Edgar Cayce. He had done his homework.

Sara, too, was eager. In a way, Edgar Cayce's work had become the key to her determination not to give up completely on the possibility of reincarnation. If she was ever to have her "love for the ages," she simply had to be sure that James was her soul mate. And that meant maintaining her belief that she had shared a previous lifetime with him—which in turn meant that reincarnation would have to be true.

During the week, James had called Sara about 4:30 one morning. He had been out partying. They talked for over an hour, and it was like old times. Naturally, James' call only made it that much harder for Sara to give up on the soul mate idea. Never mind that James had said he was still going out with

Diana. For Sara, the mere fact that he called was as good as a shooting star in the astrological charts.

Nor did it help that Tina had picked right up on James' call when Sara told her about it. According to Tina, the timing of James' call coincided precisely with her meditations, which had told her something dramatic was about to happen in their relationship.

This was the first time Sara had hidden anything from Eric since they began meeting. She was sure she already knew what he would say. Nor, for the same reason, had she told Tina about her discussions with Eric. Sara was still caught between two radically different worlds.

———— ◆ ————

"There's that smug look again," Sara teased as Eric sat down.

"I'm sure you're right, though I promised myself I'd try to hide it today. I know how much you admire Cayce."

"It's not so much that I admire him," Sara said, seeking the right nuance, "it's just that he presents such a strong case for reincarnation. First of all, here is a man who was once a Sunday school teacher and still believed in the Bible. Whatever else he may have been, he was always a Christian.

"Then, there were all those healings—something like 30,000 case histories. They weren't the same as what happens with some of the faith healers. No one was throwing away his crutches or walking away from his wheelchair to the applause of the audience. Who's to know if those people needed the crutches or wheelchairs in the first place? With Cayce the process was always the same, and always carefully documented. He would go into a trance, be given the simplest information about the person who was ill, and immediately give a correct diagnosis and prescribe the appropriate cure. Now that's what I call credibility."

Eric knew in advance that this would be the hard part. From what he had read, there was little room for maneuvering on this aspect of Cayce's life. "What can I say? From what I can tell, your 'Sleeping Prophet' had a pretty good batting average when it came to healing folks. I can't explain it, nor can I really deny it. This much I'll just have to concede."

"But see, that's the point," Sara said with growing confidence. "If his healings are verifiable, then what he did in his so-called life readings takes on credibility.

"You won't believe this," Sara said, poking fun at her own lack of Bible knowledge, "but I actually found a Scripture passage that I was looking for last night!"

"Well done! We'll make a real Christian out of you yet," Eric grinned.

"It's in John 10:37,38." Sara had placed a marker in her Bible so she could turn to it without fumbling. "It's Jesus talking about his miracles: 'Do not believe me unless I do what my Father does. But if I do it, even though you do not believe me, believe the miracles, that you may know and understand that the Father is in me, and I in the Father.'"

She looked up. "I'm not suggesting in the least that Cayce is on the same plane as Jesus, but I got to thinking about the matter of authenticity and credibility. Jesus' miracles were his badge of authenticity. If people were having trouble believing his teaching, he could always point to his miracles as proof that he had the moral authority which he claimed."

"You're right, of course. But there are two important differences between Christ and Cayce, wholly apart from the fact that Jesus was the Son of God. First of all, Jesus' miracles were just that—*miracles*. Apart from the one time when he had that blind guy put mud on his eyes, I don't remember when Jesus ever resorted to anything like a home remedy. Shucks, even the mud didn't fall into that category. Jesus' miracles were always *instantaneous* and *supernatural*.

"Second, Jesus' teaching was just as credible as were his miracles. You can't point to anything Jesus ever said that contradicts history, or shows him to be saying something to stroke his own ego, or catches him in some contradiction. Of all the things that Jesus' opponents ever said about him, they couldn't fault the integrity of his teaching."

"Are you suggesting that Cayce's life readings are somehow flawed in this respect?"

"Yep, big time!"

Sara took a deep breath. She knew Eric had been eagerly awaiting this moment. He had told her last week that he had even gone to the Bodhi Tree himself to get more books on Cayce. Leave it to her to pick a sounding board who would take his assignment so seriously!

"As you know, Sara, these so-called life readings were similar to the healings. Cayce would go into a trance, be given the name and perhaps the address or birthdate of the person seated by him, and then he would tell them all sorts of things about their supposed past lives. Sometimes in his trances he even talked about his own past lives, or the lives of various biblical characters. A secretary would write down whatever Cayce said, and those records became the basis for all the Cayce books that have been published."

"How many did you manage to read?"

"A *bunch*! I've had Cayce on my brain for over two weeks now. But it's been kinda fun, really. Sort of like going through depositions and getting ready for cross-examination."

Sara prepared for the onslaught of Eric's research. "Fasten your seat belts, ladies and gentlemen," she said mockingly, "the pilot is revving up to take off!"

"Okay, here goes. First of all, didn't you find it curious—even suspicious—that so many past lives in his thousands of life readings turned out to be related to *Cayce's own* supposed past lives?"

"I really didn't notice that many, but I might have just missed them. Or maybe it was more obvious in the books you read that I didn't."

"Then, of course, there were all those readings supposedly revealing that Cayce's friends and associates were previously famous figures in history."

"You mean like, who was it, Cayce's nephew?"

"His *secretary's* nephew."

"Yeah. Didn't he turn out to be Alexander the Great?"

"*And* Thomas Jefferson! Why is it that in your past lives you're never an ordinary fisherman on the banks of the Zambezi River? You're always some well-known historical personage or at least in the entourage of some famous king or pooh-bah!"

"That's not always true. Tina never gave me any exotic past-life pedigree. And I don't think James was any conquering hero."

"You can count your lucky stars she didn't!"

"What was that?" Sara counterpunched with delight.

"Oops. This New Age stuff is invading my brain!"

"Tell me about Cayce's own life readings. My books didn't really go into those."

"Cayce had a lot of past lives—too many to go into now. But here's one I thought might interest you. It supposedly took place about a thousand years after Adam. Cayce incarnated as the Egyptian high priest Ra Ta. During this incarnation, Cayce was instrumental in building the Great Pyramid. Nice work, Edgar. But look at this account of that period." Eric turned the book so that Sara could see the paragraph he had highlighted.

Sara read it aloud. "The Egyptians, in their cultural advancement over Arart's more pastoral and simple tribesmen, had long enjoyed lighter-than-air travel in gas-laden balloons introduced to them by the Atlanteans in times past. Ra Ta saw an opportunity to visit other areas of the world where the sons of men were gathered. So he went to India, to the Gobi land, to Og, and to what is now Peru, as well as to Carpathis . . ."

"That's good," Eric interrupted. Here's the point: Supposedly in his former life as this Egyptian guy, Ra Ta, Cayce visited the lost continent of Atlantis. One of his interpreters, Gina . . . Gina Cerminara . . .

says of this particular reading, 'If the Cayce readings are to be accepted, Atlantis did very definitely exist.'

"Of course, you can turn that around just as well— and *should*! Because if Atlantis did *not* exist, then neither are Cayce's readings to be accepted as true. Given the lack of any evidence that Atlantis ever existed apart from mythology, I'd say the verdict goes against Cayce."

Sara tried not to reveal her discomfort. "I'll withhold my verdict until the end of the trial, counselor."

"Here's another one. 'As a soldier of Troy, Cayce helped defend the main gate of the besieged citadel. When the city fell, he was so humiliated that he committed suicide.'

"Maybe his tragic demise accounts for the mistake in dates which Cayce obviously made in the reading. His reading—and I checked; it was not just a subsequent recording error—his *reading* indicates that he lived as the Trojan soldier from 1158 to 1012 B.C., a period of 146 years!

"Now I know that Methuselah lived for 969 years, but in the days of Troy I don't think anyone was living to be 146!"

"Eric, you're incredible," Sara said with a mixture of resignation and admiration.

"I discovered that neat little tidbit about 2:00 the other morning. We stodgy lawyer-types have to get our cheap thrills some way!"

Eric repositioned himself, as if preparing to launch a final salvo. "I gotta tell you, Sara, our friend Cayce comes awfully close to blasphemy when he starts talking about the supposed incarnations of Jesus, before he was Jesus. That wasn't in any of the books you gave me, was it?"

"No, unfortunately. Or perhaps fortunately."

"Well, according to Cayce, Jesus incarnated as the biblical Adam, somewhere around 12,000 B.C. The implication that Jesus, therefore, was the one who committed Adam's sin was not lost on Cayce. Check this out. It's reading #2067-7.

'Q-3 *When did the knowledge come to Jesus that He was to be Savior of the world?*' 'When He fell in Eden.'

"So Jesus our Savior, says Cayce, committed the original bad karma!"

"Ouch!" Sara reacted.

"There's more to come. But . . . oh . . . before I get to that, check this out." Eric flipped quickly to another page.

"Here's another great Eric catch," he said with a twinkle in his eye.

Sara loved watching Eric when he knew he was onto something. He was like a little boy excitedly opening a Christmas present, with ribbons and wrapping flying in all directions.

"Cayce's readings said that Jesus also incarnated as Enoch—remember, the guy who didn't die but was taken up into heaven? Of course this means that Cayce messed up yet again, because *both Adam and Enoch were living at the same time*! Although Enoch was born many years after Adam, Adam was still alive at the time of Enoch's birth, making the two of them contemporaries!"

Sara could only smile. "Split personality, perhaps?"

"Right! And now for a bit more blasphemy. Cayce said that Jesus also incarnated as Zend—the father of Zoroaster—whose own father was Uhjltd, supposedly Cayce himself in a former lifetime. Look how interestingly that works out: Uhjltd (Cayce) is the father of Zend (Jesus). *Jesus the only begotten son of Cayce?* A bit presumptuous, don't you think?"

"Just a tad."

"And I guess it was all this cosmic closeness which gave Cayce the insight to know something the rest of us were never told—that, when Jesus finally incarnated *as Jesus* and was condemned to death, he—so says Cayce 'joked on the way to Calvary, as He carried His own cross.'"

Sara gasped. "Did Cayce really say that?"

"'Fraid so, my friend."

Eric sat back. He decided not to bring out some other good stuff he had on Cayce. He figured he had already dropped enough bombs—maybe too many. Sara was looking pensive, and casually picking at her fingernails.

"I don't mean to rub it in," Eric said apologetically.

"No. No, that's fine. It's what I asked you to do, to help me get a better perspective on what I've been reading and thinking. It's just . . . it's just that I had invested a lot in Cayce."

"So, it seems, has everyone else in the New Age movement," Eric ventured. "Doesn't Shirley Mac-Laine feature Cayce prominently in her books?"

"Yes. And at the Bodhi Tree, there's an entire section of Cayce-inspired books. He's sort of the George Washington of New Age."

"Why do I have the feeling that Cayce would have told a different story about the cherry tree? Or maybe, just maybe," Eric suggested impishly, "Cayce *was* George Washington!"

Sara barely acknowledged Eric's attempt at humor. She just shook her head slowly back and forth. "I don't know, Eric. I mean . . . I don't know. I just don't know."

For a long time they sat in silence—two people separated in background and perspective but bonded together by a struggling search for truth.

———— ◆ ————

Sara broke the silence with a surprise announcement. "You're not going to believe what I've done."

"What's that?"

"When I was at the Bodhi Tree some time ago, I saw a flier for a channeling session with Kevin Peterson, the famous psychic that all the movie stars go to. It's next Thursday night, and I signed up for it."

"Say *what*? You signed up for a psychic channeling session?"

"Yeah. Remember that dream I told you about when we first met? The one Tina said was a clear sign that James and I would be married within two years and live together 'throughout eternity'? Well, I thought the channeling session would be a good way to backstop Tina's interpretation—you know, to see if Kevin gives it the same interpretation. He's going to be interpreting dreams for the group that night."

Eric became instinctively protective. "Are you prepared to be disappointed? I mean, what are you going to think if he *doesn't* confirm what Tina said?"

"Then maybe it will be just one more nail in my New Age coffin." Sara paused, wishing she hadn't said anything.

"Eric, I know you must think I'm crazy, but I've got to know for sure. I've just got to know."

"No way I can talk you out of it?"

"You're sweet, but I'm afraid not."

Eric thought about it for a minute, then made his own surprise announcement. "Okay, I'm going with you."

"You're *what*?"

"If it's not too late to sign up, I want to go with you."

Sara was aghast. "Aren't you afraid of treading on dangerous ground? Doesn't it reek of witchcraft or something?"

"That's precisely why I want to go along. It *is* dangerous! I don't like the thought of your going alone."

"But I'd feel terrible if you got yourself into something you didn't feel comfortable with."

Eric thought about it again. "I tell you what— maybe someone needs to do an undercover investigation. Remember that class I was telling you about at my church? Last week someone asked about spiritual warfare, and satanic stuff, and demons. I was 'volunteered' to lead the discussion at the end of the month. So I'd love to know if this channeling business is demonic, or if it's just a snake-oil show.

"Yeah . . . yeah . . . the more I think about it, the more I think it's worth investigating. Most of all, though, I'm convinced that you oughta have a spiritual bodyguard."

"Okay, Mr. Secret Service! I'll sign you up. But don't say I never warned you."

"I'll be frank with you, Sara. I'm already convinced that *all* psychics, Tina included, are doing the devil's business. I think the whole New Age phenomenon, from crystals to tarot cards, from astral projections to hypnotic regression and Cayce's life readings, are all part of Satan's domain. I don't have to see Kevin's act to know that much. But I *am* curious as to whether demons actually speak through the channelers like they spoke to Jesus during his ministry.

"My initial suspicion is that they are just high-priced con artists. Who knows? After Thursday night maybe I'll file a class-action suit against Kevin for fraud against the public, and then give the money to recovering guru-holics."

"Guru-holics? Eric, you're hopeless!"

A serious look came across Sara's face. "I have to admit that the possibility of demons did cross my mind. I may be into lots of crazy things these days, but I'm definitely not into demons!"

Sara looked at Eric. "Now that I think about it, I'm glad you're going with me. I just might need a spiritual bodyguard after all."

Then Sara quickly flashed back to their earlier discussion. "Edgar Cayce was different in that regard, wasn't he?"

"Well, at least Cayce never claimed to have any other 'entity' speaking through him. It was always his own person and voice speaking. These other guys are like human telephones. If you can believe them, they vacate their bodies and loan them out temporarily to highly evolved spiritual beings on the astral plane who are networked with the Akashic Records, or 'the Universal Mind,' as they are sometimes called."

Sara had just been reading about the Akashic Records. "They're like a psychic computer bank, aren't they? Supposed to have a complete file on everybody and everything?"

"Exactly. So you can ask these cosmic computer operators anything you want—about health, romance, past lives, future lives—whatever. For 50 bucks you have omniscience at your fingertips. Everything, that is, but what the stock market will do next Monday, or which horse will win the third race at Santa Anita. If these guys were as good as they say they are, they'd all be filthy rich!"

"Of course, you know their answer to that. Psychic powers should never be used for personal material gain."

"Yeah, right! Just how much are they charging for their services?"

Sara reached over and patted Eric on his arm. "Easy, boy, easy."

"So how will you know if it's demons at work or simply Kevin?" she took up again.

"I don't know. I'm hoping it's like what Justice Stewart wrote in one of his opinions about pornography: 'I may not be able to define it, but I can recognize it when I see it.'"

"Well, I hope you're right. I can accept the possibility that there is psychic power to tap into, but demons I don't need."

"Me neither," said Eric. "Before we go to the session, I'm gonna be on my knees, praying for God's protection."

"Would you mind if I joined you when you pray?"

Eric looked deeply into Sara's eyes. He was delighted at her suggestion. "You're on, my friend. I've got a feeling God has something very special in store for us."

Sara suddenly sat up. "Something special in store for us?"

"Yeah. You know. He may have some really important lessons to teach us."

"Yes, of course." Sara looked away, letting her mind wander.

8

♦

*Testing
the Spirits*

Eric and Sara drove up to the house just before 8 P.M., and parked across the street. They were surprised that such a well-known psychic as Kevin Peterson would be holding his channeling sessions in an ordinary home in the suburbs. They watched as several people, mostly unaccompanied women, arrived in BMW's and Mercedes Benzes and went inside. They were casually but smartly dressed, as if attending an informal dinner party.

Eric turned to Sara. "Would you like to have one more prayer before we go in?" Sara nodded.

They joined hands and bowed their heads.

"Father, we thank you that we can call you our father. We praise you for having created us in your likeness and for having called us in love to be your children. As we've come to you in prayer over these last few days, so we come now once again, aware that we need your strength, your wisdom, and most of all your protection.

"You know our hearts, Lord. We come not to seek

answers from him who rebelled at your authority before the world began, nor from his legions of demons. We know that Satan is the father of lies. But on Sara's behalf we have come to test the spirits. Fill us with discernment that we may clearly distinguish between the purity of your truth and anything false.

"Father, I ask especially that you give Sara the clarity and peace which she seeks. Let her find rest from all her struggle. I thank you that you have given her a searching mind, but most of all I thank you for her honest heart. May your truth be revealed in her heart, and in every way may this night be to your glory. For we ask these things in the name of him who is truth, Jesus our Savior. Amen."

"Amen."

It was time to go in.

———— ◆ ————

"Welcome. I'm Rhonda Feldman," said the woman at the door. "I believe you are the last two that we expect. Please come in and make yourselves comfortable in the living room."

Rhonda turned out to be the owner of the house, and was a gracious hostess throughout the evening.

About 20 or so people were scrunched together in the front room, some sitting on couches and chairs, others on the floor. A large overstuffed chair had been reserved for Kevin, who suddenly appeared— to the obvious delight of his small audience—with the kind of flair normally associated with actors. Eric wondered if Kevin's flair for the dramatic had come from his much-touted association with movie stars, or—more interesting yet—whether Kevin himself were an actor by training.

With all eyes riveted on him, Kevin plopped down in the chair and then flashed a broad boyish smile. He was dressed in tan slacks, brown leather loafers, and a bulky tan sweater. All in all, he clearly looked the part of a rather bohemian spiritual adviser. Even his eyes were dark and mysterious.

"Why do all these psychics have dark, mysterious eyes?" Eric asked himself. "If eyes are windows to the soul," he thought again, "maybe I've got my answer. It's probably the kingdom of darkness that they are reflecting!"

"I want to welcome you all this evening," Kevin began. "It should prove to be a fun occasion."

That's all it took to infuriate Eric. "Fun occasion?" he said to himself, as if screaming back at Kevin. "You're getting ready to deceive these folks and give them false spiritual information, yet you call it a 'fun occasion'?"

"What I think we will do tonight," Kevin began, "is to divide the evening into two parts. In the first part, I will try to give you an overview of spiritual intuition from such diverse fields as religion, psychology, science, history, and philosophy. It is important that we understand the nature of the soul and of true reality before we proceed further. That should take about an hour, and then we'll have a break.

"After the break, I will enter the trance state and allow you to inquire of Spirit whatever may be of interest to you. However, as advertised, tonight we want to concentrate our energies on your dreams and their interpretation. All right?"

Kevin then launched into a fascinating lecture on the psychic world of the paranormal. He lived up to his own billing, drawing from a wide variety of fields to explain the meaning of life from a mystical, spiritualist perspective. Eastern religions were given significant attention, with Buddha drawing special honor. Taking their place alongside Buddha were Freud, Carl Jung, and many other well-known philosophers.

It didn't take long to appreciate that Kevin was not to be compared with your local palmist or crystal ball mystic at a two-dollar-entry-fee psychic fair. He was bright, well-read, articulate, thoughtful, and, for all appearances, sincere. His smile was truly infectious, and his self-deprecating humor added to his seeming credibility. Quite simply, Kevin was someone whose knowledge, innocent charm, and genuinely likable personality made you *want* to believe him.

Laced throughout his informal lecture were repeated references to Jesus, whom Kevin described as "the most highly evolved soul to ever have lived." At one point Kevin described himself as a "Christian reincarnationist," coming from a mixed Presbyterian and Baptist background. But it was clear that Kevin's was an all-inclusive religion, or better yet a cosmic spiritism transcending traditional religions of any stripe.

Much of what Eric and Sara were hearing was familiar territory. They recognized most of the concepts from the New Age books they had already read. But never had they heard New Age philosophy so clearly and succinctly articulated.

When Kevin stopped for the break, neither Eric nor Sara could believe the hour had gone so quickly. Their minds were still racing. It had been like Mr. Toad's Wild Ride trying to assimilate the breadth of ideas Kevin had covered. At the same time, they were desperately trying to sort out fact from fiction.

What they were beginning to appreciate fully for the first time was that the line between fact and fiction is never more elusive than with New Age teaching. Their first clue might have come from all the emphasis Kevin put on the Hindu concept of *maya*. In Hindu thinking, *reality itself is illusion*.

Eric wondered, How could they be sure that they even existed, or were in that very room that moment listening to Kevin? And how could Kevin claim to know truth, when truth itself would be only an illusion?

——— ◆ ———

As Kevin disappeared upstairs, Rhonda invited everyone to get up and stretch. Soon the kitchen became the hub of activity, with herbal tea and various juices being offered. Rhonda introduced Eric to a new culinary experience: rice cakes, peanut butter (unprocessed and unsalted, of course), and honey.

"You're dripping, counselor," Sara said as she reached up to wipe away a drop of honey from Eric's chin.

"*Gracias*. So what do you think so far?"

"Quite a performance!"

"Are you using that word advisedly? Do you really see it as a 'performance'?"

"It's sure hard to tell, isn't it? I know one thing, though. Kevin's such a master at this that if I had never asked you to get involved in my psychic search, I'm sure I would be totally, *totally* taken in by it."

Eric agreed. "It's not difficult to see how people can get hooked on this stuff, particularly if they don't already know what they believe or have a strong personal faith. New Age gurus must eat people like that for breakfast! Did you see how these folks were hanging on to every word, like it was heaven-sent?"

"Yeah. Whatever else he is, Kevin is no spiritual Tupperware party, like so many I've heard about where some laugh-a-minute psychic is called in to be the entertainment for the night."

Eric was glad he had insisted on coming. "Just look around at the people who are here. Upper-middle-class, able to afford the upmarket entry fee, and mostly professionals. I'll bet we're looking at a lot of empty souls tonight. What else brings them out but a spiritual vacuum?"

Eric surveyed the crowd once again. "Kind of sad in a way, especially when you remember what Kevin said about all the truth of the universe being within us. If it's already in us, why are these folks so spiritually empty? In fact, if it's already in us, why do we have to read a small library of books or pay someone else to tell us about it?"

Sara took issue with that. "Christians don't necessarily go to church because they're spiritually empty. They're going to express the faith that's already inside them and to learn more about the

One who spiritually fills them. So why indict these folks with some lesser motive?

"And don't forget why *I'm* here," she went on. "It's not because I'm spiritually empty, but because I'm sufficiently *spiritually-minded* to take on a serious quest for true knowledge."

Eric backed off. "You may be right. I still think there's a lot of emptiness around here, but you may be right."

"Besides," Sara pressed, "how do you explain the *soul-searching* we all do? Isn't it an effort at achieving self-awareness and self-discovery? Isn't it looking within ourselves for answers?"

Eric thought for a minute. "What soul-searching I've done has never been to *find* truth within myself; rather, it's been an effort to *relate* what I see within myself to the truth I've discovered outside myself. The *truth* I get from God and the Bible. Does that make sense?"

—— ◆ ——

Before Sara could answer, Rhonda announced that it was time to go back into the living room. Kevin was already in the room, talking to a woman seated beside him. Eric and Sara took their places with great anticipation. Especially Sara, since this was the moment she had really come for.

Kevin waited for everyone to get quiet, then explained what he was about to do. He was going to enter the trance state and make way for an astral plane entity, whom he called "Tom," to take over. In his most recent previous life, Tom had been an Irish pickpocket.

Eric couldn't resist a cynical thought about a room full of people seriously seeking spiritual guidance from a pickpocket!

Kevin invited everyone to take turns speaking to Tom. They were to relate their dreams and let him interpret them. Tom was to be addressed as "Spirit."

"I'll be back with you when you are finished," Kevin said with his boyish smile at full flash.

With that, Kevin took several deep breaths, shook his head from side to side, and slumped into the big chair. A minute or so passed in silence.

"Hi there, folks. I'm Tom. Top o' the mornin' to you. Or is it top o' the evening? My cosmic clock must have missed a tick."

Eric didn't know whether to be disappointed or relieved. He was expecting a classier act from Kevin. This was sheer vaudeville! No, it was *worse* than vaudeville. "I've heard some Irishmen in my time," Eric thought, "but none of them ever sounded like this guy!"

Tom then invited everyone to share their dreams with him. The woman who had been talking to Kevin during the break started the ball rolling with her dream about an ocean voyage that ended up in Tahiti. Tom's interpretation—at least the short version—was of a spiritual journey that would take her into new understandings about herself.

"Not terribly creative stuff," Eric thought. "I could do that well myself."

One after another, dreams were told and interpreted. Even if Eric thought it was vaudevillian, those who were telling the dreams seemed to be dead serious about it. None of them seemed to be put off by Tom's fake Irish accent.

Eric occasionally glanced at Sara out of the corner of his eye. What he wouldn't give to know what was going through her head! From what he could tell, she was captivated if not convinced.

It soon came Sara's time to tell her dream, the same one she had told to Tina. "Spirit," she began nervously, "I dreamed that I was on a ferris wheel that went 'round and 'round until it stopped to let someone climb in beside me. It was my friend Bob. The ferris wheel went around one time, and Bob got out. My friend Adam then got in beside me, and the ferris wheel circled around once again. As before, it stopped after one time around and Adam got out. When my friend James climbed in and sat beside me, the ferris wheel went two times around and stopped, but James didn't get off like Bob and Adam had done. The ferris wheel started up again and went 'round and 'round without ever stopping again."

Sara then waited for Tom to react. She was about to go crazy wondering if he would confirm what Tina had said about her being married to James within two years and living with him "throughout eternity."

Tom's voice interrupted that thought. "The ferris wheel, my dear lady, represents your search for a soul mate."

Sara almost gasped out loud. (So did Eric.) "I can't believe it!" Sara's mind raced. "It's going to be the same interpretation!"

"When John first joined you in the ferris wheel..."

"Bob. It was Bob," Sara blurted out.

"Yes... when *Bob* first joined you in the ferris wheel, you thought that he would be your soul mate, but it was not in the stars. Could that be right?"

"Yes," came Sara's relieved response.

"The second man . . . his name again, please?"

"Adam."

"You also thought that Adam would be your soul mate, but I'm afraid, my lady, that he too was taken from your side."

Sara was tense with anticipation. She knew what had to be coming next.

Eric could feel his pulse quickening.

It was as if Tom sensed the drama between the two of them. There was a pregnant pause that seemed to Sara to last forever. "I believe it was James who got in next . . ."

"Yes, Spirit," Sara whispered prayerfully.

"James looks like he is to be your soul mate, but the ferris wheel goes around twice. It means that James loves two women at the same time. When the ferris wheel keeps going 'round and 'round, it symbolizes his inability to make up his mind as to which one he ought to love. Because the ferris wheel never stops, I take it, my lady, that he never decides. He is not the soul mate of either woman."

Sara's eyes teared up. Her mind was awash with conflicting emotions and thoughts. Spirit was telling her that James was *not her soul mate!* Tina had said definitely *he was.* So how could she really know?

But then, she thought, wasn't that the whole point of the exercise? Wasn't she there to see whether two different psychics could come up with the same interpretation? Maybe this was the answer she didn't want but was really looking for. Since the psychics disagreed, maybe there was nothing to this psychic stuff after all.

"I guess that's it," Sara finally said to herself. "There's no such thing as the Akashic Records or the Universal Mind that knows everything like they claim."

"But wait," she quickly remembered. "Tom was right! James *is* in love with two women. I forgot about Diana! How would he have known about Diana?" And with that thought Sara was catapulted once again into maddening confusion.

— ◆ —

Eric knew he had to make his move. An idea first occurred to him when Tom was stumbling over the names in Sara's dream, and now it was sounding better and better. The woman next to him was trying to get Tom to help her remember a dream that she had mostly forgotten. Tom wasn't having much success. His frustration was all too apparent.

"Thank you, Lord," Eric prayed silently.

The woman finally gave up her attempt. It was Eric's turn to talk with Tom, and he decided to go for it.

"Spirit," he began. (It galled Eric no end to have to use that designation. It was too similar to *Holy Spirit* for his liking.)

"Spirit, how is it that you can tell us the interpretations of our dreams but sometimes have difficulty with the dreams themselves?" Eric hoped he hadn't blown his cover.

For the first time, Kevin shifted uncomfortably in his chair. After a few moments, "Tom" came back with a response that sounded more like Kevin the lecturer than Tom the pickpocket.

"To try and extrapolate the whole dream does two things. One, it robs a person of much of the feeling if I do it for them; and secondarily it detaches a person. If they do not go through the feeling of verbal description, they may not connect with the analysis . . . because the analysis must coordinate with the feeling of a person. And thus it fatigues the instrument to extrapolate all the information. And some information is wiser not to divulge . . . it may upset the emotional applecart."

"Bingo!" Eric thought. "I've got him!"

"'It fatigues the instrument,' my foot!" Eric said to himself, mimicking Kevin's answer. "We're paying big bucks for this guy—let's wear him out!"

Eric was on a roll. "Spirit, my dream was of a plane—a jumbo jet—that was flying just 50 feet or so off the ground. It followed along a major four-lane highway for miles before breaking through a paper barrier—kind of like when football players first come onto the field and run through a banner that the cheerleaders are holding. On the other side of the paper barrier was a bright sunset. When the plane hit the sunset, it exploded."

Eric hardly listened to the generic fortune-cookie interpretation. He didn't need to. He had made up the dream as a test. If "Tom" were really in touch with the Akashic Records, he should know that the dream was a complete sham!

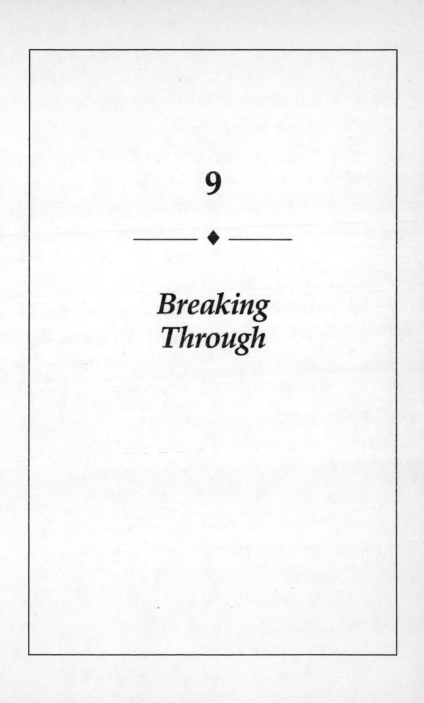

9

◆

*Breaking
Through*

B ack in the car, Eric told Sara about having made up the dream.

"Why does that not surprise me? *A jumbo jet flying through a paper barrier?* Only you could have come up with such a bizarre scenario!"

"I wouldn't talk if I were you," Eric grinned. "Your ferris wheel was *for real!*"

"Yeah, I suppose you're right."

Eric shifted the focus. "Did you catch what I was doing when I asked Tom why it was that he could interpret dreams but couldn't relate the dream itself?"

"Yeah, what was that all about?"

"I got the idea from the book of Daniel." Eric reached back and got his Bible from off the back seat. He handed it to Sara.

"Turn over to Daniel, chapter 2, I think it is."

Eric realized Sara was having difficulty finding Daniel. "It's Isaiah, Jeremiah, Ezekiel, Daniel..."

"Patience," Sara chided, "I've got it."

Eric was eager to tell the tale. "Here's the gist of the story. It seems that King Nebuchadnezzar had a dream he wanted to be interpreted. So he calls in all his magicians and astrologers to interpret the dream for him. But the king is no fool. When they ask him what the dream was, he says, 'You tell me the dream, and then I'll know you're telling me the truth about the interpretation.'

"Of course, this drives those guys crazy. They know they don't have a clue about his dream! All they've ever done is to listen to whatever dream is related to them, and then make up some hokey interpretation out of thin air.

"But ol' Nebuchadnezzar plays it tough. In fact, he tells them that if they don't tell him his dream, he'll chop 'em up, piece by piece!

"Are you in chapter 2? I think I've highlighted the good part . . ."

Sara had already located it. "Yeah, beginning in verse 9 . . .

'So then, tell me the dream, and I will know that you can interpret it for me.'

The astrologers answered the king, 'There is not a man on earth who can do what the king asks! No king, however great and mighty, has ever asked such a thing of any magician or enchanter or astrologer. What the king asks is too difficult. No one can reveal it to the king except the gods, and they do not live among men.'

This made the king so angry and furious

that he ordered the execution of all the wise men of Babylon."

"Is that great, or what?" Eric practically reveled. "I can almost see Kevin's face among the sorcerers! "Of course the end of the story is that God gives the dream and its interpretation to the faithful Daniel, who Nebuchadnezzar thereafter promotes to a prominent position in the royal court."

Sara was impressed. "You're amazing. I never read that story before. But it sure drives home the point, doesn't it?"

"I'm telling you, it's the perfect test! Did you see how uncomfortable Kevin was when I questioned him? Trust me on this—Kevin is as much a fake as Nebuchadnezzar's magicians. Guys like him have been scamming off the public for centuries. As long as there are gullible people around, you can bet there'll be someone there to take their money."

"Referring to anyone I know?" Sara asked with a knowing smile.

"Oh, I didn't mean to imply..."

"It's okay, I deserve it. I know I've been pretty vulnerable to whatever Tina directed my way. And Kevin could have put the icing on the cake if he had come through with James being my soul mate."

Sara began thinking aloud. "I'm all but convinced that you're right about these psychics. There's just one thing, though. It still bothers me that 'Tom'—or Kevin, or whoever he was—knew about Diana. How could he have known that James was in love with two women at the same time?"

"Have you never made a lucky guess? Besides, he never mentioned Diana *as Diana*."

"True, but it's pretty eerie when you think about it. How else would he have known there were two women in James' life?"

———— ◆ ————

Eric reflected for a moment and decided it was time to talk about something he had been wanting to explore in more detail with Sara. There would never be a better time.

"Sara, your use of the word 'eerie' may have been more appropriate than you might have guessed. You remember when I said I was curious to see if Kevin was channeling demons? It is possible, just possible, that that's your answer."

"Demons? You think Tom was demonic?"

"I'm not sure; nor am I sure it's *ever* possible to know for certain."

"But I thought you were laughing your head off at how hokey Tom sounded," Sara noted somewhat anxiously.

"I was, but you still never know. If Satan is the father of lies, he must also be the master of masquerade—even *poor* masquerade if that's all he needs. After all, who ever would have thought Satan would look like a *snake*?"

"But would Satan or his demons have done such a sloppy job on my dream—mixing up the names and all?"

"Why not? No one else in the room seemed to take the slightest notice. And, maybe, just maybe, God had his own helpers at work. We *did* pray for his protection, didn't we? Maybe God garbled Satan's message especially for you."

"Objection, your honor. The witness' testimony is speculative."

"Objection overruled. It is only speculative if there can be no basis in fact for the testimony.

"Turn over there to Deuteronomy 18:10."

Sara was proud of herself. She opened right to the passage. "Believe it or not, this is one passage I have been painfully aware of:

> Let no one be found among you who sacrifices his son or daughter in the fire, who practices divination or sorcery, interprets omens, engages in witchcraft, or casts spells, or who is a medium or spiritist or who consults the dead.

"But this doesn't specifically mention psychics or channelers," Sara pleaded.

"How about 'interprets omens,' as in *interprets dreams*? And, of course, it specifically says *mediums*."

"Is Kevin a *medium*?"

Eric couldn't restrain himself. "As a matter of fact I think he's a *large*! Just kidding."

"Eric, you're bonkers. No, really. Do you think he's a medium?"

"Isn't a medium an intermediary, a go-between? Didn't he claim to act as a conductor for this so-called 'Tom,' or 'Spirit'?"

"I never really thought about it that way. I just assumed he was tapping into the psychic power of the Akashic Records."

"If there *are* such records!" came Eric's retort. "But you have to look at what Kevin *claimed* to be doing, which was acting as a medium."

"But *you're* not convinced that he was ever really doing that."

"No, you're right. To tell you the truth, I get the feeling that Satan gathered his demons around him and said, 'Take the night off, gang. Ol' Kevin down there has already got them in the palm of his hands, so there's no need for us to join the party.'

"Even so," Eric carried on, "the point is that you can never know. That's why the Bible says it's wrong to take a chance. I confess I never felt very good about being a part of that business tonight. I just didn't want you going in there alone."

Sara gave Eric a look that conveyed sincere appreciation. He sensed her gratitude and looked again at the road ahead. Neither of them spoke for a mile or so.

"I think that's the spookiest thought I've ever had," Sara began.

"What's that?"

"That there was at least the possibility that we actually, literally communicated with a demon tonight. It gives me chills just to think about it!"

———— ◆ ————

"Ironically," said Eric, remembering another biblical example, "the seriousness of the whole thing is brought out in one of the funniest passages in all the Bible. Ever hear about the Witch of Endor?"

"No, I don't think so."

"It's a great story. I think it's near the end of 1 Samuel, maybe chapter 27 or 28."

Sara began flipping through the Bible to find it. "Chapter 28," she confirmed.

Before she could begin reading, Eric launched out in another of his patented paraphrases. "It seems that King Saul, in a time of spiritual rectitude, banishes all the mediums from the land. Then the dreaded Philistines come up against him, and he gets really terrified. So he tries to learn from God what the outcome of the battle will be, but God doesn't give him an immediate answer—probably because Saul himself hasn't paid much attention to God during this time!

"Anyway, not to be put off, Saul asks if there are any mediums left around, and he's told that there is this lady down in Endor who consults dead spirits. So Saul disguises himself and slips down there at night. For fear of Saul's own edict, the woman is reluctant to do her thing, but Saul insists that she put him in contact with the now-deceased Samuel.

"The funny part is this: You get the idea that she herself never believed she could really get in touch with dead spirits in the first place. Like Kevin, she was probably just a good con artist. But all of a sudden she sees the spirit of Samuel rising from the dead and she lets out the shriek of a banshee!"

"Watch the road, Eric, or we'll soon be talking to Samuel ourselves!"

"Sorry. I just love this story!"

"Couldn't tell!" she said with a smile.

"So Samuel is all upset at Saul . . ."

Sara picked up at that point. "Yeah, here it is. Samuel said to Saul, 'Why have you disturbed me by bringing me up?'"

"And that's the moral of the story," Eric concluded: "You don't mess with mediums who claim to be able to consult with dead folks—not because they're always lying to you, but because *it is seriously possible to enter the realm of the dead.* The dead are still *alive* somewhere out there, and God doesn't want Satan or his demons helping us make any long-distance calls to 'em!"

"Wow!" Sara had never thought about anything quite that mind-blowing.

Then she thought back to something Kevin had said. "Remember when that guy in the purple sweater asked Kevin if he could put him in touch with his deceased father? Kevin said, no, he didn't do that kind of thing with everyone who is dead— only with the disembodied spirits of highly evolved entities who were specially plugged into the Universal Mind."

Eric smiled. "That's undoubtedly a safe decision on his part. If he claimed otherwise, then the slightest factual blunder or difference in accent would give him away.

"However, he did say, remember, that if you have a dream and some loved one who is dead appears in your dream, then it's all for real. If they talk to you in the dream, then they *really are* talking to you!"

"Yeah, I found that interesting," said Sara, as she still skimmed the story of King Saul.

"So what do you think about dreams, Eric? Look here, verse 15. Saul is complaining that God no longer speaks to him 'by prophets or by dreams.' Doesn't that imply that God once *did* communicate with him through his dreams? And what about Nebuchadnezzar's dream? And, who was it— Pharaoh?—who had the dream that Joseph interpreted?"

"Dreams, visions, voices—God even spoke to Balaam through Balaam's ass!" Eric exclaimed with delight. "There's no question but that dreams were one of the ways God spoke to people in Bible times."

"So," Sara asked, "is it possible that God could still be speaking to us in our dreams today?"

"That's a biggie. That's a real biggie. Lots of people think so. For that matter, lots of *Christians* think so. Dream journals are not just popular among the secular crowd. But it's one of those areas where one has to exercise extreme caution.

"Theologically, the problem is that we now have the Bible in written form which contains God's final word, or as the apostle Peter puts it, "everything we need for life and godliness." In terms of spiritual truth, we don't need any other revelation, through our dreams or otherwise."

"But why couldn't God help us with more personal questions—like mine, for example—through dreams?"

"Well, of course, he *could* if he wanted to. That part is not in dispute. It's a 'given' that God has the power to break into our world with all the force that it takes to, say, bring about healing. And I believe that God is constantly working in my life in any number of providential ways. I also know for sure that he answers prayer, though not always like I want him to."

"So isn't it possible," Sara pressed, "that God could communicate 'providentially,' as you say, through our dreams?"

"Like I said, it's definitely possible. The first question is whether he actually *does*, and the second is, how would we ever be able to verify it?

"Flip back to the concordance for a minute and look under dreams. I've forgotten the passage that provides the caveat."

"The what?"

"Sorry. Lawyer talk. *Caveat* means *warning.*"

"I think it was something like Martin Luther King's famous line: 'I had a dream...'"

"Here it is. Jeremiah 23:25."

Sara turned to the passage and read aloud the verses which Eric had already highlighted.

> I have heard what the prophets say who prophesy lies in my name. They say, "I had a dream! I had a dream!" How long will this continue in the hearts of these lying prophets, who prophesy the delusions of their own minds?

"Drop down to the next highlighted verses," Eric directed.

Sara began again:

> This is what each of you keeps on saying to his friend or relative: "What is the LORD's answer?" or "What has the LORD spoken? But you must not mention "the oracle of the LORD" again, because every man's own word becomes his oracle and so you distort the words of the living God, the LORD Almighty, our God.

"See," said Eric, "that's the problem with interpreting dreams. It's always hard to know whether they are truly from God or from one's own imagination. It's like when people today say, 'God told me this or God told me that.' If it's not something you can read right out of the Bible, you're walking on dangerous territory.

"In fact, our communication with God—whatever form it takes —is not just dangerous territory, but *sacred ground*. It scares me the way a lot of Christians seem not to notice."

Sara was quick to put two and two together. "In a way, Christians have the same problem as New Agers, don't they? Once you venture into the realm of the supernatural, you're almost flying blind. If you think that God is talking to you in your dreams, you've always got to make sure that no one is on the phone impersonating his voice!"

Eric was already impressed with Sara's analysis when suddenly she ventured even further. "Maybe, too, there are some things we just aren't *supposed* to know. Or maybe we're asking the wrong kinds of questions. If I were honest about it, I'd have to admit that I've been spending a lot more time selfishly looking for my soul mate than discovering what God tells me in the Bible about my relationship with *him*."

"Well, count me in there," Eric agreed. I'm always letting things interfere with my getting to know God better. And I've even highlighted my entire Bible!"

———— ◆ ————

They turned the corner and came to a stop in front of Sara's apartment house.

"Well, my friend, it's been quite a night."

"Sure has," Sara nodded.

"So, tell me. How are you feeling?"

Sara found that to be a difficult question to answer. She took her time, and then began somewhat haltingly. "I'm . . . glad I went. It hurts a lot to . . . to think how gullible I've been. But it opened my eyes to a lot of things. Umm . . . I don't know."

Sara looked up at Eric. "It looks like I'm about to be one of your . . . 'recovering guru-holics.'"

Eric smiled warmly, tenderly acknowledging her capitulation. Deeper down in his heart, Sara's words made him leap for joy! His eyes moistened from—from what? He didn't know. Relief, empathy, admiration?

Sara looked away again. "Tina's not going to like it if I don't show up anymore. She must have thought there was no end to my curiosity—not to mention my *generosity*! But I'm convinced now. I'm convinced that Tina has no psychic power or insight into my love life. And . . . uh. . . ." Sara struggled. "I believe now that past lives are just a fantasy. *My* fantasy."

Eric didn't respond. Sara was fidgeting quietly. Eric knew that Sara was approaching the highest hurdle of all. Silently sharing her hurt, he almost stopped breathing.

"I . . . uh." Sara reached up to brush away a tear. "I know . . . uh. . . ." Sara's voice began to break. "I know that James isn't my soul mate." Her tears quickly turned to sobbing.

Sara had put off making that admission for several weeks now. In the back of her mind, she had known it. She had known it all along. But until this very moment she had kept the dreaded truth imprisoned in chains of false hope.

Eric reached for his handkerchief and laid it in her hand. Then he sat in silence, thinking that thoughts which are already known need not be spoken.

"I'm okay," she said after awhile, daubing her eyes with Eric's handkerchief and managing the slightest smile.

Sara bit her lip tightly and let out a deep sigh. "Boy oh boy . . . it's been a long journey. I thought I would *never* be able to say that!"

"Sara, you are one courageous lady," Eric said softly.

"I don't know, Eric. I think I've just been one *stubborn* lady."

Eric brightened a bit. "Do you know how many people go through life and never once ask the hard questions? My guess is, a lot! Just think how blissfully ignorant they must be! Pain and gain really do go together, don't they?"

"Unfortunately."

"Take me, for instance," Eric teased. "I know I'm a big pain, but look what you gain!"

Corny as it was, it made Sara laugh. "You're such a big pain all right. You're the only sounding board I've ever had that kept beating me over the head!"

She looked at Eric straight on. "Seriously, Eric, I want to thank you for . . . well, for everything. You've been wonderful to me."

"My pleasure, Sara. You've taught me an awful lot as well. "Now listen, are you gonna be all right?"

"Yep. I'm tough. And I also feel like I'm back in God's hand. I truly feel a sense of peace. Not like before, but *true* peace this time. A peace based on *knowledge*, not just wishful thinking."

"Good. You can rest assured I'm gonna keep praying for you."

"Thanks again. I couldn't have done it without you."

Sara leaned over and gave Eric a hug. "I'll call you tomorrow," she said as she slid over to get out.

Eric drove through the night, but he was not alone.

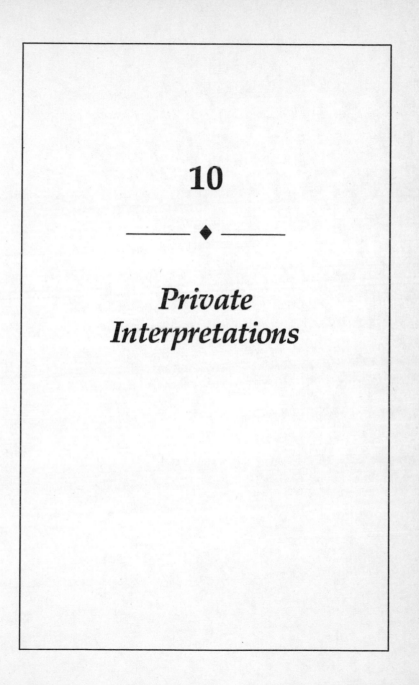

10

◆

*Private
Interpretations*

Counselor? I've been given your name by a mysterious woman with a crystal ball and a dark veil. She said I should give you a call."

"Oh, really?"

"She tells me that you are an exceptionally bright lawyer. A bit prone to insomnia, overzealousness, and corny jokes, but otherwise altogether likable."

"Well, you can tell this mysterious woman of yours that she is incredibly perceptive! Of course, she did fail to mention handsome, debonair, and frighteningly humble!"

Eric roared with laughter. "How are you, my friend?"

"Great! Really great! It's been ages since I've felt so good. It's like the proverbial load has been lifted. I've even been to see Tina, to tell her I'm not coming back."

"How'd it go?"

"Well, first of all, before leaving for Tina's place I prayed for God's strength and protection. With that, I plucked up my courage and drove over. I explained right away why I had come—to sever the relationship.

"Tina still couldn't understand why James and I were not together. I told her that I had turned everything in my life over to God, including my love life, and that if God wanted me to be with someone in particular, he would certainly be able to make it happen.

"'There is nothing else for you to do, and nothing else for me to do,' I told her. 'We simply have to give it over to God.'"

"I'll bet she loved that!" Eric chimed in.

"Well, actually, I was surprised at her reaction. She blessed me, and said it was wonderful news. 'My work is complete,' she said. Then she blessed me again, prayed a short prayer, and said, 'Go in peace.'"

"And I *did* go in peace, Eric. This is the happiest day of my life!"

"I must say it's pretty thrilling for me as well. It really makes my day to know that you're in such good spirits."

"By the way, did you tell her about Kevin?"

"No, not today. I felt I was doing good just to break it off. But I've been praying for Tina, and I intend to write her a letter, sharing what I've learned about New Age and the occult. Maybe I can get your help on pointing her to some appropriate Scriptures."

"I'll copy some of them today," said Eric as he scribbled a note to himself.

"By the way, while I was having breakfast this morning, it dawned on me that I hadn't asked you about your New Age class at church. How's it going?"

"It's really been super. Richard—the guy who is teaching it—has been studying the New Age for years. This week he's going to talk about how New Agers use—or, more correctly, *misuse*—the Bible in support of their beliefs. That's one area that I didn't read up on as much as I would've liked, so I'm really looking forward to it."

"Could you use someone to carry your books?" Sara asked coyly.

"You mean you want to come?"

"Would that be okay?"

"Of course! Great! I'll pick you up at 7:00."

"Super! See you then."

Even after Sara had hung up, Eric kept the phone to his ear. He didn't seem to notice the loud beeping sound. His mind might just as well have been on the astral plane.

—— ◆ ——

"Richard, how are you tonight?" Eric stepped across the room and shook hands with a tall, burly figure of a man. Richard was a history teacher at a high school in the valley—kind of a gentle teddy bear that all the students liked because he could transform the ancient past into living technicolor. But his gentleness belied a stormy past.

Richard had grown up in the redwoods of Northern California. His size, not to mention his limited formal education, made him perfectly suited for working as a "choker" on the same lumber gang that his father had worked for years. Like the other lumberjacks, Richard worked hard, drank hard, and fought hard.

Being a "choker" was dangerous business. If the cable around a big redwood ever snapped, the odds were that the "choker" who had manhandled it into position would be hit full force by the flying strand of twisted steel. And snap they did!

The story hardly needed telling. One day when Richard and his father were working with each other to load a particularly heavy log onto the truck, the cable slipped out of Richard's hand and whipped violently around, almost decapitating Richard's father. Richard walked out of the woods that day and never returned.

When he finally surfaced, Richard had become a marijuana-smoking, draft-protesting hippie, living in the Haight-Ashbury district of San Francisco. He hung out in the coffee shops and began reading everything from Jean-Paul Sartre, the existentialist, to Madame Blavatsky, the spiritualist. After dabbling in the Hindu Vedas, Richard began practicing Yoga and getting off on Zen Buddhism.

Only a close brush with death while hallucinating on LSD brought Richard back to reality. He cut his hair, shaved his beard, and threw away his tie-dye shirts. For a while he worked as a carpenter, but by night he struggled to overcome his deficient education.

At the local community college he met his wife, Amy, who soon led him to the Lord. The preacher said he wasn't sure Richard would fit into the baptistry, but somehow by the grace of God they managed it.

To see Richard today, you would never guess his ragtag past. He had gone on to get an M.A. in history at the University, and had become a much-demanded Bible class teacher in the church. With the growing popularity of the New Age movement, Richard had gone back and made an in-depth study of the very subjects that had so captivated him at a time when hardly anyone had even heard of the term "New Age." Now he was being invited to speak to churches all over the area, and spending much of his free time counseling former New Agers.

"Richard, there's someone I want you to meet," Eric said as they walked toward Sara. "She's the one I was telling you about who has been struggling with psychics and channeling."

"Richard, meet Sara. Sara, Richard."

"Welcome, Sara," said Richard, reaching out to shake her hand with the unmistakable grip of a former lumberjack. "I'm glad I'm finally getting to meet you. Eric's always telling me about this woman who keeps him up so late at night that he nods off during my lectures!"

"No way!" Eric protested. "I haven't missed a word. And I've got reams of notes to prove it!

"Sara, this is the 'nice guy' I was telling you about—the one who 'volunteered' me to lead the discussion on spiritual warfare."

Sara smiled at Richard. "I can't think of anyone more qualified—especially after the personal tutelage I've given him over the past few weeks!"

Richard laughed as he glanced down at his watch. "Oops. I'd better get things started. It's great having you with us tonight, Sara. Watch your friend, here, and make sure he doesn't doze off!"

———— ◆ ————

"As we announced at the last class," Richard began, "tonight we want to cover some of the biblical passages often used by New Agers in support of their beliefs. Recognizing that New Agers draw principally from the major Eastern religions, I guess the first question that comes to mind is why they would feel compelled to cite the Bible at all. Does anyone have any thoughts about that?"

"Could it be," offered a lady in the back, "that in our culture we are more familiar with the Bible than, say, the Vedas, and so there's more of a comfort zone there?"

"Yes, I think that's right," said Richard, "although we should probably use the word 'familiar' with caution. Like so many Americans today, most New Agers are not *personally* familiar with Scripture. Biblical illiteracy everywhere abounds—even among professing Christians, I'm afraid."

Sara felt the sting of that indictment, but had already committed herself to diligent study.

From over on the side, an elderly man wondered aloud if the problem wasn't that New Agers instinctively knew that somehow, someway they had to deal with Jesus. Deep down, he supposed, everybody realizes that Jesus spoke the truth and therefore is the standard against which all other beliefs must be judged.

"The sad part," Richard responded, "is that everyone wants Jesus on their side, but only on their own terms. We are about to see a number of examples where Jesus' words are twisted and turned to justify beliefs he would never have taught. In fact, let's look at the passage which is most often cited in support of reincarnation. Turn, if you will, to John 3:1-7.

"Most of you will recognize this conversation between Jesus and Nicodemus in which Jesus tells Nicodemus that he must be born again. It's the passage from which we get the popular, if somewhat redundant, phrase 'born-again Christian.'

"New Agers tell us that the rebirth to which Jesus refers is reincarnation. In fact, John Van Auken's popular New Age book is actually entitled *Born Again . . . And Again*. Can anyone see a problem with that interpretation?"

"How about what verse 6 says?" someone suggested. "'Flesh gives birth to flesh, but the Spirit gives birth to spirit.' When Jesus told Nicodemus that we must be born of water and the Spirit, he's ruling out any physical, fleshly, carnal rebirth. The rebirth he's talking about is our *spiritual* rebirth."

"Good."

A young mother spoke up. "I can relate to Nicodemus' bewilderment about being born again. Having just given birth to our second child, I shudder at the very thought of his statement in verse 4: 'How can a man be born when he is old? Surely he cannot enter a second time into his mother's womb to be born!' I'd have to say amen to that! Giving birth to a nine-pound baby is pain enough. I can't imagine having to *repeat* the experience with each child!"

The class broke into appreciative laughter—especially the mothers.

"You're right theologically as well as practically," replied Richard. "Nicodemus' observation about the improbability of a physical rebirth is pointedly intended to show the contrast between *physical* birth and the kind of *spiritual* rebirth that Jesus was describing. To suggest that Jesus was talking about even a *series* of physical rebirths or reincarnations over many different lifetimes misses the point by miles.

"In fact," Richard said as he gathered steam, "I find it ironic that those who deny that the physical universe exists except in our minds, and who pride themselves on being more spiritually enlightened than the rest of us, would give this passage such an obviously materialistic interpretation.

"Without any question, it was *spiritual* rebirth through faith to which Jesus was referring. It is this which brings a person new life in Christ. *Spiritual* rebirth is its focus.

"I can remember my own conversion," Richard reflected. "It was the beginning of a whole new relationship of trust and commitment to Christ. Given my former life of sin and spiritual deadness, I can tell you I felt like a *new person*—in the same bulky body!"

Sara leaned over and whispered to Eric, "I'd love to sit in on a discussion between Richard and Kevin!"

"Yeah, me too." Eric whispered back. "Maybe we should invite Kevin to the class!"

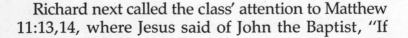

Richard next called the class' attention to Matthew 11:13,14, where Jesus said of John the Baptist, "If you are willing to accept it, he is the Elijah who was to come." He then had them read from Matthew 17:11-13:

> Jesus replied, "To be sure, Elijah comes and will restore all things. But I tell you, Elijah has already come, and they did not recognize him, but have done to him everything they wished. In the same way the Son of Man is going to suffer at their hands." Then the disciples understood that he was talking to them about John the Baptist.

"New Agers often interpret these two passages as if Jesus were saying that Elijah was reincarnated in the body and personality of John the Baptist. Does anything in the context suggest how you might respond to that assertion?"

"Well," someone ventured, "this conversation follows immediately upon their return from the Mount of Transfiguration, where they had just seen Moses and Elijah in a miraculous appearance. It would be strange, to say the least, for the disciples to have confused their contemporary, John, with Elijah, the prophet of old."

"If your analysis is correct—and I think it's excellent—what do you think Jesus meant when he referred to John as being Elijah?"

A sports junkie in the class drew from his own field of interest: "Wouldn't it be like when a sportscaster says of some outstanding young baseball player, 'He's another Willie Mays, or a Hank Aaron'? No one would understand him to mean that the kid *is in fact* Willie Mays, just that he is *like* him."

"That's a great analogy, Steve. Clearly, Jesus was merely indicating that John's *ministry* was reminiscent of Elijah's."

Eric thought of another passage that had a bearing on the discussion. "We might also want to consider John 1:19-21, where the priests and Levites asked John point-blank, 'Are you Elijah?' John's answer was an unequivocal 'No, I am not!'"

"Good point, Eric. But I have to admit I've always been intrigued that the religious leaders would have asked such a question of John in the first place. Does it mean that there were those among the Jews who believed in something like reincarnation? Or simply that God had miraculously put Elijah back on earth —original body and all? Either way, Eric's point is well taken. Any way you look at it, John the Baptist was not simply a reincarnated manifestation of Elijah.

"Incidentally, I think it's significant that, in all the New Age literature that I've read, there has never been a single reference to John's denial—only to the highly inventive interpretation of what Jesus said about him."

Sara quietly nudged Eric. "Interesting about the appearance of Moses and Elijah, isn't it? It's kinda like when Saul asked the woman to call up Samuel from the dead. The dead *do* still exist out there somewhere, *don't they!*"

Eric thought for a minute, then whispered back, "The sad irony is that, for all the wrong reasons, New Agers believe that more than many Christians seem to!"

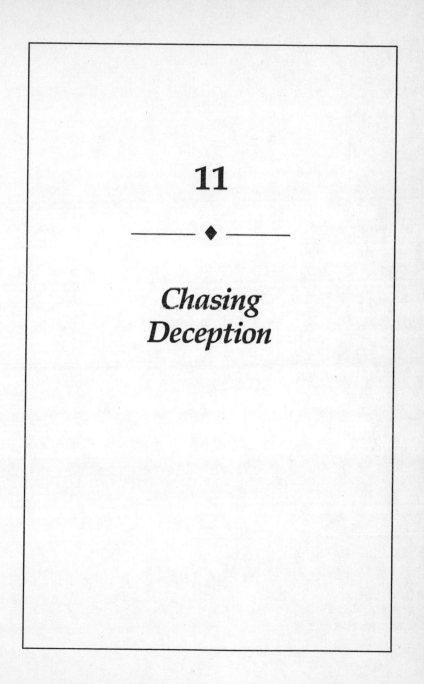

11

♦

*Chasing
Deception*

Sara looked around her in the class and couldn't help but draw comparisons with Kevin Peterson's channeling session. That night, all eyes and ears had been on Kevin: Kevin the personality, Kevin the entertainer, Kevin the guru.

In this class, by contrast, Richard was merely a backdrop, a facilitator of a mutual learning process. As well-studied and informative as he was, he himself was not the source. Like Kevin, Richard too was a channeler of sorts. But what Richard channeled was nothing more than truths emerging from the pages of Scripture, copies of which were in the hands of each student in the room. They could read, and study, and decide for themselves whether what Richard was saying was true.

The sound of pages flipping back and forth from one Scripture to another throughout the room seemed to mock the "hidden mystery" on which New Age thought prides itself. No wonder New Age needs to have its gurus! When the mystery of the universe is "hidden," only those who are fortuitously enlightened can enter the rarefied atmosphere of cosmic truth.

As never before, Sara was beginning to realize that, in Christ Jesus, the nature of God and the meaning of our existence is—if still a sublime mystery—at least no longer one that is beyond the reach of mortals like herself. Eric would later refer her to the close of Paul's letter to the Romans to confirm what she now only intuitively sensed:

> Now to him who is able to establish you by my gospel and the proclamation of Jesus Christ, according to the revelation of the mystery hidden for long ages past, but now revealed and made known through the prophetic writings by the command of the eternal God, so that all nations might believe and obey him—to the only wise God be glory forever through Jesus Christ! Amen.

"The only mystery left," thought Sara, "is why so powerful a God as the Creator of the universe would stoop down to tell me *anything*, much less that he *loves* me! Who am I to deserve that, especially after seeking answers from storefront psychics and flirting with witchcraft?"

——— ◆ ———

Richard shuffled his notes and began to shift the focus slightly. "Now then, we've talked before about the concept of karma, in which it is believed that one's conduct determines his state in the next lifetime. According to Hinduism and Buddhism, a person can actually *devolve* to a lower level, as well as *evolve* to a higher one. Hence the belief that you can come back in subhuman form as—say—a rock, a frog, or a tree. That's why, even today, the Jains over in India wear gauze masks over their faces so that they don't accidentally inhale tiny creatures who might be one of their ancestors.

"Naturally, that aspect of reincarnation doesn't play well to a Western audience, so in New Age thought, one seldom comes back as anything subhuman, and is almost always upwardly evolving. Perhaps the most notable exception is Shirley MacLaine's serious assertion that she was once an elephant."

"She *did* put that in one of her books, didn't she?" Sara remembered with renewed amazement.

"Whatever the particular details," Richard explained, "karma is basically a matter of cause-and-effect. How you live in one lifetime supposedly causes some particular effect in another lifetime. And that thought brings us to yet another passage that is often quoted by New Agers. All throughout their literature are references to Jesus' statement 'As a man sows, so shall he also reap.'

"Let me suggest one problem with that statement while you are thinking whether there is still another problem with it. The first problem is that Jesus specifically taught that there is no *necessary* cause-and-effect in play throughout the universe.

"We all know, of course, that cause-and-effect does operate on many levels. For example, the person who drives his car recklessly is liable to 'cause' an accident, which itself is the undesired 'effect.' And as those of you who are students know, failure to study is an open invitation to bad grades. So it's true that in the ordinary affairs of life, we *do* usually reap what we sow.

"But it's foolish to think that every 'effect' has a traceable 'cause.' Jesus tells us, for example, that God 'causes his sun to rise on the evil and the good, and sends rain on the righteous and the unrighteous' (Matthew 5:45). And there was also his reference in Luke 13:4 to the 18 people who died when the tower in Siloam fell on them. 'Do you think they were more guilty than all the others living in Jerusalem?' Jesus asked rhetorically, plainly indicating that no spiritual cause-and-effect was involved."

Richard took it one step further back. "Of course, Solomon had made the same point centuries earlier when he said in Ecclesiastes 9:11 that time and chance happen to us all."

Richard chose his next words carefully. "I know that some Christians frown at the use of such phrases as 'How lucky I am' or 'What a stroke of bad luck that was.' But if we are to believe Solomon and Jesus, accidents *do* happen, and bricks *do* fall off buildings without having been specifically nudged by the hand of either God or Satan. There is nothing like surefire karma even in *this* life, much less from one lifetime to another."

Sara leaned toward Eric and said quietly, "I don't know. I gotta believe it was more than luck that I 'just happened' to remember you that night while I

was tossing and turning. What do you think?"
Eric nodded.

———— ◆ ————

"I don't want to belabor this whole matter,"
Richard said almost apologetically, "but there is one
passage we simply can't ignore at this point. It's
found in John chapter 9. New Agers frequently cite
this passage as further proof of previous lives."

Sara was reveling in all the Scripture references.
She was excited to finally learn more about the
Bible. "Why were we never encouraged to study the
Bible in my own church?" she wondered regretfully.

Richard read out the first two verses:

> As he went along, he saw a man blind
> from birth. His disciples asked him, "Rabbi,
> who sinned, this man or his parents, that
> he was born blind?"

"In Jesus' day, the Jews did not believe in reincarnation, but many Jews did believe that sin was
inherited from one's parents, despite Ezekiel's re-
markable rebuttal to that idea in chapter 18. Also,
due to a misinterpretation of the Old Testament's
emphasis on perfection as a reflection of God's
glory, they often associated physical imperfections
as signs of sin, whether inherited or perhaps even
committed while still in the mother's womb!"

Eric leaned over to Sara and said, "Judging by
your looks, both you *and* your parents must be perfect!"

"Go away," Sara whispered in mock reprimand.
But his words had hit an unfamiliar target. It struck

her that this was the first time Eric had seemed to take any notice of her. She had to force herself to concentrate on what Richard was saying.

"Jesus' response to their speculation about the blind man was, in effect, 'You are wrong about that.' Look at verse 3: 'Neither this man nor his parents sinned,' said Jesus, 'but this happened so that the work of God might be displayed in his life.' Jesus then healed the man, thereby demonstrating his deity and his divine authority over creation.

"Frankly, folks," said Richard with all the bearing of his huge bulk, "I am mystified that New Agers would even bring up this passage for consideration, much less offer it as proof. Far from teaching reincarnation, it demonstrates that Jesus *specifically renounced* the idea that a person's state in this life is dependent upon anything from either someone else's life or from some previous lifetime of his own.

"Jesus' teaching is plain on its face. 'Whose sin caused this man to be blind?' they asked. Jesus responded, in effect, 'Blindness is not caused by anyone's sin. Your belief in a cause-and-effect relationship here is simply wrong.'"

Richard eased up before getting too carried away. "Has anyone come up with the other problem associated with Jesus' statement that 'As a man sows, so shall he reap'?"

Eric raised his hand. He had spotted the problem from the very first mention of the statement. "Yeah, the biggest problem is that Jesus never even said those words!"

"That's absolutely right," said Richard. "Go ahead and tell the class the proper source of that statement, and read the context for us if you have it."

"It was the apostle Paul in Galatians 6:7-9." Eric already had his thumb on the page:

> Do not be deceived: God cannot be mocked. A man reaps what he sows. The one who sows to please his sinful nature, from that nature will reap destruction; the one who sows to please the Spirit, from the Spirit will reap eternal life. Let us not become weary in doing good, for at the proper time we will reap a harvest if we do not give up.

"Good catch, Eric. I knew I could count on you." Sara gave Eric a look that asked incredulously, "How did you *know* that?"

Eric just smiled and shrugged his shoulders, feigning innocence.

"And not only do they wrongly attribute Paul's words to Jesus," Richard continued, "but they also miss an opportunity to appreciate the sublime beauty of eternal life. The eternal life that Paul is talking about couldn't be more different from reincarnation's dismal prospect of endless future lifetimes spent on this mortal coil with all its suffering, pain, and death."

It did not escape Sara's attention that the passage did indeed have something important to say about cause-and-effect. She was inwardly stirred by the thought that having eternal life in heaven won't be a matter of chance—that how we live in this life very definitely will have eternal consequences.

As she thought further about it, she was also impressed with the difference between the fake

"Spirit" that Kevin claimed to channel and the genuine article, God's own Holy Spirit. Having come so close to falling for the counterfeit, it was only the *true* Spirit whom she now wanted to please more and more each day.

———— ◆ ————

Richard held aloft a copy of Shirley MacLaine's popular autobiography, *Out On a Limb.* "I just want you to be aware," said Richard, "of the callous disregard for Jesus' teaching among many New Agers. I recognize that all too often we Christians are guilty of taking Scriptures out of context to support this doctrine or that, but I can confidently say that New Agers have made an art form out of scriptural abuse.

"Take, for example, this conversation that Shirley has with her spiritual mentor, David. David says to Shirley, 'To know yourself is the deepest knowledge of all. Christ said it: "Know thyself." And then be true to it.'"

Richard was visibly indignant. "Christ never said that! Nor did Paul or any other Christian writer. Such me-generation selfism couldn't be more in opposition to Christian teaching.

"As you may realize, 'Know thyself' is a well-known ancient Greek admonition inscribed upon the Delphic oracle and attributed variously to Pythagoras, Socrates, Plato, or others long before Jesus lived. How in the world did Shirley or her editors think they could get away with that obvious miscue?

"And as incredible as it may sound, David's last comment is an obvious paraphrase of Polonius' line,

'To thine own self be true,' in Shakespeare's *Hamlet*!

"How can we possibly put any trust in those who claim access to divine knowledge through channeling and other psychic powers, yet can't even attribute famous quotes to their proper source?"

Eric offered a legal-beagle postscript: "There's an interesting parallel here. One of the jury instructions often given to jurors says, 'A witness found to be intentionally false in part of his testimony is to be distrusted in other parts of his testimony.'"

"If the jury is still out on the New Age movement," Richard extended that thought, "then I wouldn't want to be a New Ager when the verdict is returned. Nor can I imagine the Judge of all Creation looking mercifully upon such blatant misuse of his revealed Word.

"As we do each week, let's open up the class now for any questions you might have."

"Yes, Richard," said a woman in a green turtleneck. "I was talking with a co-worker at my office the other day. She's read stacks of New Age books, and believes anything they say. But she was telling me almost the opposite of what we've been talking about tonight. She claims that the Bible once *did* teach reincarnation, but that the Catholic Church didn't like that belief and took out all the passages that referred to it. Is there any truth to that?"

"Our budding lawyer over there will appreciate this argument. As Eric could tell us, lawyers have no difficulty arguing two alternative theories, hoping that the jury will buy at least one of them."

"Make that two *completely contradictory* theories, if necessary!" Eric added quickly.

"And that's exactly what's going on here," Richard said with the confident experience of having heard this argument many times before. "Usually people are so biblically illiterate that New Agers can easily fool them into thinking that the Bible actually teaches reincarnation. But when they run into people who know their Bibles, they have to take a different tack.

"At that point it's, 'Oh, yes, you're right. The Bible doesn't *in its present form* teach reincarnation, but it *once did!*' They try to tell us that . . . well, here, let me just read an excerpt from *Out On a Limb*." Richard quickly scanned through the book and found a passage which he had marked for future reference on this very question.

"David is telling Shirley about the church's alleged Reincarnation Watergate—

> The theory of reincarnation is recorded in the Bible. But the proper interpretations were struck from it during an Ecumenical Council meeting of the Catholic Church in Constantinople sometime around 553 A.D., called the Council of Nicea. The Council members voted to strike those teachings from the Bible in order to solidify Church control. Anyway, that's what I believe Christ was really doing and when the Church destroyed those teachings, it screwed up mankind from then on.

"Tragically, we have here another example of a wanton disregard for truth. As a student of history, I can assure you that the Council of Nicea was convened by Constantine in A.D. 325, not 553. The council which met in A.D. 553 was the Fifth Ecumenical Council, known as Constantinople II. At the later council several issues were under discussion, but none dealt with reincarnation.

"What New Agers are mistakenly seizing upon is the issue raised by the teaching of a third-century theologian named Origen. Origen speculated that the soul was *preexistent*—not that it had experienced previous incarnations, but only that it had existed prior to a person's birth."

Sara was just about to ask herself how anyone could be "preexistent" when Richard explained it.

"In his earlier works, Origen had taught that humans had once been *angelic* creatures, and, in karmic fashion, were affected in this life, depending on whether they had been bad or good in their *angelic* existence. But Origen rejected both *previous* incarnations and *future* incarnations."

Richard reached into a file folder and pulled out a slightly crumpled Xerox copy. "It's a bit scholarly, but you might find this quotation from Origen interesting on this point. Ironically, he is commenting on the very passage in Matthew that we previously discussed concerning the alleged reincarnation of the prophet Elijah in the person of John the Baptist:

> In this place, it does not appear to me that by Elijah the soul is spoken of, lest I fall into the dogma of transmigration [reincarnation], which is foreign to the Church of God and not handed down by the Apostles, nor anywhere set forth in the Scriptures. For observe, [Matthew] did not say, in the 'soul' of Elijah, in which case the doctrine

of transmigration might have some ground,
but 'in the spirit and power of Elijah.'"

Richard looked out to the class and extended his upturned hands. "What can I say? By pointing— even erroneously—to the controversy over Origen's teaching, New Agers have provided the very ammunition that shoots down their own assertion that the Bible once taught reincarnation. Writing at least 70 years before the Council of Nicea and some 300 years before Constantinople II, Origen himself indicated that there was no concept like reincarnation in either the Bible itself, the apostles' teaching, or the church!"

The class seemed to erupt with ideas in response to Richard's explanation.

"The church must not have done a very good job of ripping out the reincarnation passages," commented one man wryly. "If the intent had been to rid the Bible of reincarnation teaching, then why did the church leave in all those passages we just discussed that supposedly teach reincarnation?"

Richard smiled. "Like the sowing-and-reaping passage, and the one about Elijah and John the Baptist. Good point. Anyone else have a comment?"

From a woman on the first row came the observation that it would have been a really weird Bible originally if, at the same time, it contained references to reincarnation on one hand and resurrection, heaven, and hell on the other.

From somewhere in the back another young woman observed that, if verses of Scripture *had* been removed, there would be noticeable gaps in the biblical record today—none of which appear.

"As you are all indicating," Richard concluded, "once you begin to chase the deception surrounding the New Age's attempt to draw support from the Bible, the fraud of it all is simply too glaring to miss."

Eric slid his Bible over to Sara and pointed to Hebrews 9:27. She had just read it when Richard asked, "As we wrap up our class tonight, can anyone tell us a Scripture we can use to show what the Bible *does* say about reincarnation—a Scripture which, by the way, I can assure you is never found in any of the New Age literature?"

Eric nudged Sara. "Yes," she answered eagerly. "In Hebrews 9:27 the writer says, 'Man is destined to die *once*, and after that to face judgment.'"

"Perfect," Richard said, fairly beaming that it was Sara who had come up with that important Scripture. "So next time you have opportunity to discuss the Bible with a New Ager, keep that Scripture foremost in your mind. Remember, Hebrews 9:27. Hebrews 9:27. Hebrews 9:27.

"What was that Scripture?" Richard asked with pretended forgetfulness.

"*Hebrews 9:27!*" the class responded in unison.

"Right!" said the consummate teacher, ironically employing the use of repetition in combating the false notion of the soul's repeated existence.

"We'll continue next week as indicated on the course syllabus. Are there any final announcements before we close with prayer?"

Almost everyone had left when Richard finally

was free to join Eric and Sara. "Do we have another Bible scholar in the making?" asked Richard, with reference to Sara's surprise contribution to the class.

Sara laughed and pointed at Eric. "Well, I can't lie to you. The Bible Answer Man, here, had just shown me the passage when you asked about it. But I *do* remember it was *Hebrews 9:27!*" she said with a winsome smile.

Richard's massive superstructure shook with laughter.

12

◆

*Catching
Her Act*

H ello?"
      "It's me, your knight in only-slightly-tar-
nished armor."

"I don't remember seeing any tarnish, counselor."

"Just try rubbing me the wrong way, and you
might!"

"Gag! What a horrible pun!"

"Sorry. So how'd you like the class last night?"

"It was truly awesome! Richard is so sweet and
sincere—and obviously well-prepared. But what I
liked most was just getting into the Word. I felt like a
kid in a candy store with all those verses to look up
and digest."

"It won't be long before they'll be calling *you* the
Bible Answer *Woman*," Eric laughed, remembering
what she had called him the night before.

"I doubt it," Sara protested; "you've got too much
of a head start on me."

"Say, listen," Eric suddenly changed directions,

"you're not going to believe what happened when I got into work today."

"What?"

"Well, I was up in the library, knee deep in research, and in walks Marty Brewster. He's the partner in the firm I was telling you about, remember? He and his wife are the ones who are into New Age in a big way."

"Oh, yeah."

"One day last week he took me to lunch and, naturally, we got to talking about New Age. He couldn't believe that I thought it was total nonsense, and of course I couldn't believe that anyone as bright as he is could think that it was anything *but* nonsense!"

"Really!"

"Anyway, he asks me this morning, 'Are you and your friend still reading up on New Age?' When I said yes, he handed me two reservations for Shirley MacLaine's 'Getting In Touch With Your Higher Self' seminar down at the Biltmore this weekend. Guess how much the tickets cost?"

"I dunno."

"Three hundred bucks each!"

"You're kidding! So aren't they going?"

"No, he's got to go to New York to take depositions, and Meg decided she'd rather take in a show on Broadway than catch Shirley's act here.

"So what do you think? Would you like to see Shirley up close and personal?"

"That'd be fab! At 300 dollars a person, there won't be all that many people there. We'll have great seats!"

Just then another thought dawned on Sara. "But if there is just a small in-crowd, she's going to know we're not one of her groupies. What will we do if she spots us as New Age impostors?"

"If she gets curious and asks, we'll just tell her what we believe. Who knows? Maybe the Lord will give us an opportunity to share the gospel with Shirley."

"Wouldn't that be incredible!"

Eric quickly skimmed over the brochure that came with the tickets. "This is weird. The instructions say we're supposed to wear jogging outfits and bring pillows."

"Sounds good to me," said Sara, bounding with enthusiasm at the prospect of seeing in person the famous actress whose New Age beliefs had captured the attention—and souls—of millions.

Sara wondered at the irony: Did she have Shirley to thank for having a closer walk with the Lord? After almost succumbing to Shirley's New Age teaching, Sara had found truth on the rebound. And in that truth, a *real* peace with God.

—— ◆ ——

The sign in the hotel lobby said: "Getting In Touch With Your Higher Self Seminar—Grand Ballroom."

"Hmm. That's interesting," Eric mused. "Why would such a small gathering be meeting in the Grand Ballroom?"

It didn't take long for Eric to get his answer. When they entered the double doors, instead of the cozy gathering they anticipated, there were *hundreds of people*! In fact, Eric overheard one of the ladies at the registration table say there were 800 people registered.

When Eric got over his shock, he did a swift bit of calculating. "Let's see, 800 times 300 dollars a person is . . . 240,000 dollars. Wow! Close to a quarter of a million! And this is only one of 14 seminars she's having across the country. That's . . . that's over three million big ones!"

Sara could hardly believe her eyes. "And New Agers talk about how much money Christian televangelists rake in!"

———— ◆ ————

Since it was obvious that they wouldn't be sitting on the front row, Eric and Sara decided to sit toward the back of the huge ballroom so they could better observe the reaction of the audience. There were no chairs anywhere. People were sitting wherever there was space on the floor.

Eric and Sara plopped down on their pillows and got comfortable. Relaxing wind-chime music was playing, and several people here and there were sitting in the lotus position, meditating.

"Kinda relaxing, isn't it?" Eric observed.

"Yeah, especially with that great music. Which raises an interesting question," Sara said after a moment's reflection. "Is the 'New Age music' everybody's playing these days connected in any way to the New Age movement and its beliefs?"

"Well, from what I can tell, yes and no. As for the 'yes,' all you have to do is look at those people out there who are meditating to the music. At the least, it's conducive to the kind of meditation generally associated with Eastern religions.

"As for the 'no,' surely it doesn't mean that everybody who listens to 'New Age music' is all of a sudden going to find themselves in the lotus position!"

"I don't know," Sara teased. "The music's playing, and you've already got your legs crossed in front of you!"

Eric smiled, then got a serious look on his face. "I'll tell you what I find interesting. Remember when we were talking the other night about the concept of monism?"

"Monism? Oh, yeah, the belief that everything is part of the oneness of the universe. That you are one, and I am one, and God is one, so in a strange kind of way you and I are God?"

"That's it. Well, what I find interesting about 'New Age music' is its monotonal quality. For all the 'harmonic conversions' they talk about, there's hardly any harmony in so-called 'New Age music.' If you were asked to come up with some kind of music to express a belief in monism, then 'New Age music' would certainly fill the bill.

"And there's something else. The typically repetitive theme of the melody in 'New Age music' reminds me of reincarnation. I'm sure it's coincidence, but it's interesting, isn't it?"

Sara mulled that over in her mind, and then realized there was yet another curiosity. "Have you ever thought about the fact that 'New Age music' is almost entirely instrumental? I mean, there's never any lyrics. Isn't that odd?"

Eric had never thought about it before, but it occurred to him that even that made sense. "Maybe it's because they really don't have a story to tell. With Christian music, in particular, we've got the greatest story ever told!"

The more Eric thought about it, the more he liked it. "You know, that's got to be right! Pagan music has always been more instrumental than vocal. If you don't have a story to tell, all you can do is play!"

———— ◆ ————

At last, there she was on the stage, looking bigger than life, just like on the silver screen.

"Wow, she looks great!" Sara thought enviously. "I only hope that I look half as good as that when I'm her age."

Eric was impressed with her mind. Everybody talks about Shirley as if she's a nut case, but that could only be with regard to what she *believes*. Eric could tell that, as a person, Shirley was extremely bright. And as he thought about it, she would have to be bright to be such a good actress.

More than her intelligence, Eric had to admire her breadth of knowledge—at least with regard to New Age and occult teaching. Shirley had lectured for almost two hours, covering much the same material as Kevin Peterson had presented—and all this without a single note! Whether it was karma and reincarnation, or chakras, or astral projections, Shirley was right on top of her material.

At the first break, the audience gave Shirley a standing ovation.

———— ◆ ————

The room was completely silent, and 800 people hardly breathed. Eric and Sara looked deeply into each other's eyes. Deeply, in a way they had never done before. At first they had smiled, as if it were a game. But their smiles were soon replaced with piercing intensity.

Shirley had directed the audience to pair off—with complete strangers, if necessary—in order to perform a series of relaxing exercises. It would help prepare them for a more important exercise to come, she said.

Each couple was to sit facing each other. Then each partner was to rub his or her hands together until the friction had created a noticeable warmth. At that point the two people were to put their hands next to each other's, as if they were playing patty-cake, but—Shirley was explicit—the hands were not to touch!

"Feel the energy passing between you," Shirley said. "Can you feel it? Our souls are energy. When energy is exchanged, the souls are free to inter-mingle.

"Now look your partner in the eyes. Look deeper. Even deeper. What can you tell about your partner? Have you known your partner in past lives? Who were you then? Were you related in some way? Were you perhaps lovers?"

At that, Eric wondered if something were not off-kilter. He had noticed that the overwhelming majority of participants in the seminar were women. That meant most of the partnered "couples" were both women. "Did that last question about being past-life lovers strike them as odd?" Eric mused.

But then a passage from *Out On a Limb* rushed into his mind. In the passage, Shirley's personal channeler had just told her, through an entity known as "John," that in a particular period of her many past lives she was reincarnated twice as a male and once as a female. Shirley's curiosity drives her to ask:

> "Could that be a metaphysical explanation for homosexuality? I mean, maybe a soul makes a rocky transition from a female to a male body, for instance, and there is left-over emotional residue and attraction from the previous incarnation?"
> "As such," said John, affirmatively.

"For anyone who is seriously into reincarnation thinking," Eric thought, "maybe that question wasn't so odd after all!"

However, at this moment Eric's philosophizing was ancient history. All he could see was the beauty and brightness of Sara's eyes. Through her eyes, he reckoned, surely he was looking at the most wonderful soul he had ever known. Did his own eyes reveal what he was thinking, he wondered with a tinge of embarrassment?

How could he have known that Sara was thinking the exact same thing! Neither of them said a word, or moved, or dared to breathe. Their hands were so close, their eyes so fixed, their hearts so melded together.

Shirley's voice suddenly broke the silence. "For our next exercise, I want you to take turns massaging each other's shoulders. Massage is an important part of Oriental philosophy. It stimulates the circulation and thus the body's aura of energy."

Carefully following Shirley's directions, Eric and Sara took turns massaging each other's shoulders.

"Now *this*," said Eric, "is worth the price of admission!"

"Especially since someone else paid your 300 dollars!" Sara smiled. And with that, she pressed harder with her thumbs.

The other 798 people in the room that day might as well have been on Jupiter. New Age or no New Age, Eric and Sara were in a cosmic orbit all their own.

———— ◆ ————

Shirley called everyone's attention to the front and dived into another aspect of her lecture. "We need to take on personal responsibility for our lives. Skepticism is a limiter, and fear is a governor. We must rid ourselves of fear."

"Who could disagree with that?" Eric thought. "But when does the other shoe drop?"

It dropped just as he was finishing that thought. "We choose everything that we experience," Shirley assured the audience. "We participate in every way every day with what happens to us. There is no good or evil except as we create it. We each create our own reality. Therefore we must learn that there are no victims!

"If, for example, a couple learns that their newborn child has been born physically handicapped, it should be a comfort to them to know that the child has chosen to be born handicapped, and that they themselves have chosen to have parented a handicapped child."

Sara gasped and looked at Eric with disbelief!

Eric was somewhat surprised, but not shocked. His shock had come a few days earlier while reading the book entitled *Ramtha*, allegedly the recorded conversations of a 35,000-year-old Hindu warrior channeled by J. Z. Knight, a former mentor of Shirley MacLaine's. (Ramtha's claimed age had hit Eric as extremely funny, since Hinduism itself is not that old!)

But Eric had found nothing funny about the conversation between Ramtha and a person called "Master":

> *Ramtha:* There is no such thing as evil. Since everything is a part of God, if you were to say that any one thing is evil, you would also be saying that God is evil, and he is not.
>
> *Master:* So you don't even think that *killing* someone is evil?
>
> *Ramtha:* That is correct.
>
> *Master:* So you're saying that even murder is not wrong or evil.
>
> *Ramtha:* That is correct. Each entity perceives what will be good for his being. That is his option, that is his choice.
>
> If an entity is moved to slay another, the entity *needs* to experience that for his purposeful understanding. And I wish you to understand that the entity who participates with the slayer in his expression is not the victim of the slayer. For perhaps he has contemplated the possibility of being burned, or cleaved in two, or molested.

Thus the one who needs to slay and the one who needs to be slain draw each other together for the experience.

Eric shuddered even at the memory of what he had read! And here was Shirley, affirming the same basic concept of value-neutral, personally created reality.

"It's all a matter of choice," Shirley said confidently. And then she paused and smiled. "For example, I have chosen to be rich!" The audience laughed and applauded, as if to affirm in their own minds that they too could be rich if they would only choose it for themselves.

Sara leaned over to Eric during the applause and said, "So what does that say for all the poor and starving people in the world? Did they *choose* their miserable existence?"

Eric shook his head in shared consternation.

Shirley was not through with this line of thinking. "We need to affirm that we have taken control of our lives. When you wake up each day, do as I do. Call them mantras, if you will, or merely affirmations. Whatever you call them, they'll make you feel good."

It was here that Shirley took the most dramatic departure of all. "Affirmations are spoken resolutions which, when used properly, align the physical, mental, and spiritual energies. The ancient Hindu Vedas claimed that the spoken words *I am*, or *Aum* in Hindi, set up a vibrational frequency in the body and mind which align the individual with his or her higher self and thus with the God-source. The word 'God' in any language carries the highest vibrational frequency of any word in the language. Therefore, if one says audibly *I am God*, the sound vibrations literally align the energies of the body to a higher atunement.

"You can use *I am God* or *I am that I am*, as Christ often did, or you can extend the affirmation to fit your own needs."

Sara looked at Eric. Eric looked at Sara. They had read this same message in Shirley's books, but it still hit home with full force when it came from her own lips.

They were not prepared at all for what came next.

"The reason we have control of our lives, the reason we must choose our own reality, is that we are not simply human beings as we tend to think of ourselves. Our humanness is a limiting thought. We are not mere mortals."

Shirley gave a dramatic pause, looked straight out to the audience, and delivered the coup de grace: "As Jesus and Buddha have said, 'Be still and know that *you* are God!'"

At that blasphemous utterance, Eric's first impulse was to get up and leave. He knew all too well what apparently no one else in the ballroom knew, or cared to know—that those words were a 180-degree perversion of Psalm 46, in which God is speaking and says, "Be still and know that I am God; I will be exalted among the nations, I will be exalted in the earth."

Shirley had just put herself in dangerous jeopardy of God's wrath! It was *Shirley MacLaine herself* that she was exalting, not the Mighty God of the universe who had created her and imbued her with an intelligent mind and extraordinary talent.

"God forgive her!" Eric prayed silently.

———— ♦ ————

In all his reading of New Age literature, Eric had constantly wondered if New Agers *really* thought of themselves as God, as they so often said.

For example, there was that classic exchange between Shirley and her friend David who kept tutoring her on New Age thinking. In the television adaption of *Out On a Limb*, they were on the beach at Malibu. Shirley kept hounding David with one question after another. Finally he turns to Shirley and tells her that all the answers are within her. Why? Because she is God. When Shirley feigns hesitation, David urges her to come right out and say it.

At first Shirley rather timidly says, "I am God." Then David encourages her to say it again and again. Finally she turns to the ocean, spreads her arms out wide, and shouts for the heavens to hear, "I am God! I am God! I am God!"

Eric remembers having said to himself, "You can count on it, Shirley; the heavens *did* hear you!" But he still wondered whether her idea of God was the God of the Bible. Maybe she had a different definition or concept of God.

One of the Cayce-inspired books that Eric had read with interest had offered a far more fanciful explanation of God: In the beginning, so it seems, there was a sleeping, slumbering ball of energy known as God Force. God Force is all there was. And it was energy. But God Force roused itself, and when it did, it exploded—in Big Bang fashion—into billions and billions of points of consciousness, each one of which was still part of the God Force.

And that, according to the book, was where we come in. Each of us, said the author, is one of those points of consciousness, or what we call a "soul." Since each soul was once a part of God, then each soul still *is* God.

The problem is, the book went on to explain, that we have lost the vision. We are metaphysically ignorant about our divine god-ness. It seems that these "points of consciousness," or souls, gradually started coming down into the three-dimensional earth plane; and when they did, they forgot that they were God. Instead of thinking of themselves as *infinite*, they began thinking they were *finite*. When they should have known themselves to be *immortal*, they settled for *mere mortality*.

Eric's lawyerly curiosity questioned how the three-dimensional earth plane itself came into existence, but no explanation was ever offered. What Eric did pick up on was the supposed role of reincarnation. The purpose of our many incarnations, supposedly, is to help us come to the awareness that we truly are God. Always were. Always will be.

"We are God, and this life is only an illusion?" he thought with curious incredulity. Eric had been dumbfounded at the thought that we were supposed to come down repeatedly into a three-dimensional earth plane in order to learn the lesson that the three-dimensional earth plane did not exist in the first place!

When Eric had shared that cynical observation with Sara, Sara had taunted him, saying, "You're simply being too rational, counselor. You'd better face the fact that the karmic computer in the astral plane is going to sentence you to a thousand more lifetimes so that you can shed your blinding rationality!"

———— ◆ ————

At that very moment Shirley was turning her attention along similar lines. She was reaching the point where the title of her seminar, "Getting In Touch With Your Higher Self," would begin to take on meaning. She explained that we have two selves: our higher self and our lower self. Our higher selves are transcendent, having learned the lessons of the soul's many reincarnations. It knows that we are God. By contrast, our lower selves are still metaphysically confused, and therefore they have difficulty acknowledging that we are God.

Sara thought to herself, "If the higher self already knows what the lower self has yet to learn, then why the charade of further cosmic education for the lower self? It's as meaningless as an adult saying, 'I need to become a baby again so that I can learn to have the adult awareness that I already have!'"

Even as Sara was wondering how Shirley would respond to her observation, Shirley said that the moment had come for them to get better acquainted with their higher selves.

"Maybe this *is* Shirley's response," Sara thought.

"I want all of you to relax," Shirley began. "We're going to take the most important trip of your life, to meet your higher self."

Shirley then had everyone close their eyes and imagine a fanciful flight of the soul. "Let yourself feel lighter and lighter until you feel like you are floating out of your body. Up you go, higher and higher, until you are flying alongside the birds. Isn't this *fun*?" she exulted.

She took the audience by their imaginations into outer space and told them to look back to the earth—which, she suggested, they could visualize as the blue-green terrestrial ball now made so familiar by photographs from moon-walking astronauts.

"Now come back down again... slowly... ever so slowly. Back down to where the earth gets larger and larger. Aim for that large green area over there. Slowly now... descend very slowly. You will see that you are coming down into a garden, a lush green garden with foliage all around you.

"There is a large opening in the garden. Do you see it? Let yourself come gently down into that opening, and, almost hovering, let your bare feet touch down into the cool mud of the path that you see before you. You may begin to walk now. Just go straight ahead, past those fernlike leaves which are reaching out to caress you. Look up ahead, now. There's a babbling stream in front of you, and a bridge crossing it. Go up on the bridge and feel the coolness of the spray from the water racing beneath you.

"As you leave the bridge, the path quickly leads to another large opening in the garden. Do you not sense that you have finally arrived at your destination? In point of fact you *have* arrived," said Shirley with the kind of excited anticipation that only a top-class actress can create.

"There straight ahead," Shirley said, as if opening the envelope before an expectant Oscar-night audience, "is a large tree. And standing at the foot of the tree—however you conceive it to be—is your higher self.

"Let me introduce you to your higher self. Your higher self is the one to whom you have been praying. Your higher self is the one who has been answering your prayers. Your higher self is God!"

———— ◆ ————

The reaction around the huge ballroom was unbelievable. At the moment Shirley introduced the audience to their higher selves, there was clapping, and weeping, and joyous whooping—all mixed together in a cacophony of sounds.

Eric and Sara just looked on, amazed and bewildered. They had tried to join in the visualization exercise just to see where Shirley was going with it, but they were too far removed from the process for it to affect their emotions like seemingly everyone else.

What had these people seen at the foot of the tree? Who or what had they visualized as their higher selves?

Sara thought it was interesting that Shirley had tied the higher-self concept to prayers and answers to prayers. Did that take people back to the God of the Bible rather than the God Force of New Age? New Age literature hardly ever mentions prayer.

And did this mean, Sara wondered, that people had all along been praying to *themselves*? "Have we bowed in our weakness to what turns out to be our own weak selves?" she questioned critically. "And if our higher self is God, then what need do we have of prayer? If we are God, why are we not all-powerful and all-knowing? If we are God, why do we need Shirley MacLaine to introduce us to ourselves!"

Eric himself was off in a different direction. He could not help but think of the similarities between what he had just witnessed and the events surrounding the first sin. Just as at the dawn of creation, Shirley's introduction to higher self had taken place in a *garden*, and the focal point had been a *tree!* "Was that not the setting for the very first deception?" Eric asked knowingly. Did not Adam and Eve's sin involve the seductive thought that they too could become God?

That thought lingered as Eric watched Shirley leave the stage and slowly snake her way through an admiring audience to the side exit.

13

◆

Instant Replay

Y ou did *what*? You actually went to Shirley's seminar?"

Richard was clearly envious—not because he was any fan of Shirley MacLaine, but because he had done so much research into the New Age movement. Listening to Shirley's presentations would have been the icing on the cake!

Eric and Sara simply smiled, as if they had just filed an exclusive story under the nose of the competition.

Richard and his wife, Amy, had invited Eric and Sara into their modest home for lunch after church. "Let's have our prayer, pass the food around, and then hear all about it," said Richard, playing the respective roles of patriarch, host, and dedicated New Age watcher.

When their plates were filled to overflowing with Amy's finest roast beef and potatoes, first Eric, then Sara, recapped the seminar in vivid detail. Richard begged them not to skip a thing. His eager curiosity explained how he had become so well-informed on the movement.

From time to time Richard would break in with a question. "How did the audience react when Shirley told them there was no such thing as good and evil because we each choose our own reality?"

"That's what amazed me," said Sara. "I didn't see a soul squirming on that one. And her buildup to it was so obviously shallow! It was all that monism stuff: Since everything is part of the oneness that exists throughout the universe, there can be no essential difference between light and dark, hot and cold, good and evil. Everyone just sat there . . . as if it were some profound truth. I'm not sure they would have taken any notice if the lights had been turned off and the room become dark!"

"I think," said Eric, "it's because we all want so desperately to believe that we ourselves are the judge of what is right and what is wrong—especially if what we want to do is *wrong*. Under those circumstances it's awfully reassuring to be told that right is wrong and wrong is right!"

"And it fits so nicely with 'creating our own reality,' doesn't it?" Richard added. "We all want to be in charge of our lives—to be in control. The more our government intrudes into our lives, computer technology keeps tabs on us, and freeways crowd us in, the more we crave personal control."

Amy was normally a shy woman who preferred to sit back and listen to others, but now a thought struck her. "Isn't it ironic that we feel absolute panic at 37,000 feet because some unknown pilot is up in the cockpit with *his* hands instead of *ours* on the controls, but quite at ease when we finally land, then get behind the wheel of our own car on some crowded freeway where the chances of our getting killed are about a zillion to one compared to airplane accidents! As long as we think we are in control of our lives, we seem to be oblivious to whatever danger might exist."

Richard let out a hearty laugh. "Yep, we may have died on the freeway going home from the airport, but *at least we were in control when it happened!*"

"More scalloped potatoes and green beans, anyone?" Amy offered. The bowls and serving dishes made the rounds of the appreciative guests. It was obvious that Amy had honed her cooking skills over the 20 years of their marriage.

"That's what's so tragic about New Age," Eric said, bringing the analogy full circle. "It's people who have no control over circumstances in their lives that are attracted to New Age. They're looking desperately for some way to get a handle on their lives. Then they're told that they are God, and therefore have complete control over everything that happens to them!

"But they're *not* God, and they *don't* have control over everything that happens to them, so how can they possibly escape further disillusionment and frustration?"

"Speaking as someone who almost got totally converted to New Age thinking," said Sara introspectively, "I think a lot of people are attracted to it not so much for gaining some kind of Godlike control over their circumstances as for finding answers to questions that no one else, including the church, can provide.

"You see, if Shirley were actually right in saying that we create our own reality, then whenever we face difficult questions which seemingly have no answers, we can just *make up* answers."

Eric supplied the obvious commentary: "If logical answers let us down, our intuitive imaginations never do."

"That's how I got hooked," Sara continued. "When I got no solid answers about my love life, I was willing to fall for the most bizarre explanations offered to me, even if it meant coming to believe that James and I had shared a previous lifetime together.

"I know it seems weird, and from this distance I can hardly believe someone as normally rational as myself could ever get that far, but I know it can happen. It did to me!"

Richard was struck with Sara's words "normally rational." For a long time now he had been fascinated with the fact that so many "normally rational" people could buy off on the obvious irrationality of New Age beliefs. Yet he had always tempered his observation with the awareness that Christians also have to suspend rational thought at the point of faith.

What about miracles? he had wondered. And particularly Jesus' miraculous birth and resurrection. Surely those events aren't readily acceptable by the purely rational mind. The proof of that fact was the overwhelming number of rational people who rejected those supernatural events even in Jesus' own generation.

And, after all, what is the difference between what Christians would call "supernatural" and what New Agers refer to as "paranormal"? Ezekiel's wheel, Peter's vision, Paul's "third heaven," healings, tongues, prophecy—even Jesus' virgin birth and bodily resurrection from the tomb. What could have been more "paranormal"!

But Richard also knew there was a difference between the reasoned faith of Christians and the typically blind faith of New Agers. Christian faith is coherent, based upon solid historical evidence. There were witnesses who were willing to die, if necessary, that the truth might be told. New Age belief, thought Richard, is neither coherent nor historical. Had anyone ever died to defend the existence of UFO's and extraterrestrials, or some out-of-body experience?

In fact, as he had pointed out to his class, New Agers find it necessary to distort history and fudge on the truth in order to make their belief system work.

Amy's pouring of more iced tea got Richard's full attention back to the conversation, and again he joined in. "You know, Sara, those words you said 'normally rational'—I think they are a key to understanding how New Age has proved so successful, despite its often outrageous claims, whether it be UFO's and extraterrestrials or silver cords and astral projections. New Age has managed to convince people that rationality itself should be abandoned. How else are they going to get people to believe it?"

"And, of course," Eric chimed in, "all the trendy right brain/left brain terminology is thrown in to make it happen. New Agers tell us that we need to get away from left-brain, masculine, rational thinking, and turn to more right-brain, feminine, intuitive thinking."

Sara picked right up on the implication. "Does that mean that women are inherently more irrational?" she asked with a teasingly sinister little glint in her eye.

"I don't know about that," Eric said with something else altogether in mind, "but I can tell you that I've been entertaining some pretty irrational thoughts lately." He smiled slightly and gave Sara a quick little wink. "You reckon it's all this talk of New Age . . . or maybe something else?"

"Oh . . ." said Sara, tilting her head and squinting one eye as if seriously pondering a response, "maybe your mind is taking a little rest while your heart is working overtime."

Eric liked that word picture. More than that, he loved Sara's quick mind. And tender heart. And smile. And laugh. And . . . touch. He could still feel her hands on his shoulder, gently massaging every sinew of his soul.

Amy caught their glowing glances, and it took her back to a soft summer's eve when she and Richard had walked hand in hand by the river which bordered the campus. "Isn't love's first bud exquisite?" she reminisced to herself.

Richard was oblivious to the subtleties of their exchange. Romance, for Richard, was not on the front burner. He was still intrigued by the thought that New Age had made irrationality respectable by elevating intuitive, sensory perception over "normally rational" thought.

— ◆ —

"So what did Shirley say about Jesus?" Richard wanted to know.

"Pretty much the same thing she said about him in *Out On a Limb*," Eric responded. "You know, about the missing 18 years and all."

Richard shook his head. "It's just incredible that anyone would dare suggest that the unchronicled years in Jesus' life were spent in India, and Tibet, and Persia, and who knows where else! No doubt Jesus' fame had spread far and wide. And no doubt every religious sect in the world would want to claim a piece of the Wonder Worker from Judea. But to seriously suggest that Jesus became an adept Yogi? And that it's his training as a Yogi that explains the miracles he later performed during his ministry? Give me a break!"

"Eric and I were talking about that on the way back from the seminar," said Sara. "We were thinking how strange it would have been for those supposed far-flung travels never to have been mentioned by any of Jesus' family or neighbors. If Jesus had in fact been gone from their midst for 18 years, surely they would have blown the whistle on him."

"Yeah, I was telling Sara that, when Jesus was being charged with blasphemy by the Jewish leaders, it was *not* for being into Eastern mysticism, but for claiming to be the promised Messiah. In fact, one of the arguments offered in support of the charge of false impersonation was that Jesus had been among the local townspeople from his youth onward! 'But we know where this man is from,' they insisted; 'when the Christ comes, no one will know where he is from.' They weren't about to believe that the carpenter's son from down the road was the Messiah they had all been looking for!"

Richard nodded again and again. "It's the same song, second verse. In order to believe in New Age, you really do have to park your mind, not to mention everything you've ever learned about history."

Amy reached over and put her hand on Richard's bulky arm. "I never thought about it that way before, Richard," she said with a cute little twinkle in her eye. "If New Agers ever take over, you're out of a job! Who's going to want some oversized, slightly balding, but terribly handsome historian confusing the facts!"

Richard had not lost all sense of romance. He leaned over and gave Amy a tender little kiss. "When that happens, do you know of any petite, slightly graying, but terribly beautiful woman who might want to take him in?"

"I just might," said Amy, as if she had just been swept up into the arms of her lover.

Sara reveled in the scene, thinking how wonderful it was that two people could be so happily married. She could count on her fingers the number of happy couples she knew. By contrast, the love she could sense between Richard and Amy confirmed what she had known all along: It wasn't some past-life *soul mate* that she wanted, but a loving *life mate* in Christ.

Eric interrupted her reverie. "Sara, when you were spending time at the Bodhi Tree, did you ever read Janet Bock's *The Jesus Mystery*? Wasn't that the one that talked about the supposed secret life of Jesus between the ages of 12 and 30 before he began his ministry?"

"Yes, that's the one," said Sara. Even back then she had thought it was all highly speculative—more like fables or interesting hypotheses. But the more serious threat, Sara was beginning to understand, was the way in which Jesus, *as Christ*, had been compromised.

"Don't you think," Sara asked of Richard, "that the more subtle deception is the way in which Jesus, *as Christ*, is presented? To be frank, I'm still not completely sure about what Shirley and other New Agers mean when they refer to '*Christ consciousness*.' Tell me again what that's all about."

Richard stretched his huge frame as if preparing for a formal presentation. Amy picked up the plates and headed for the kitchen.

"To get to 'Christ consciousness,'" Richard began, "I need to give you a really quick summary of three different theologies."

Eric leaned forward, knowing that they were in for something good. Sara was ready to scribble his ideas on a mental notepad.

"The first one we're already familiar with. Christian theology says that God created the universe and all that's in it. Unlike in paganism, God came before nature, not the other way around. And he was a God with personality, not just energy or force.

"When God created man, he made man in his own image and longed for fellowship with him; but man sinned and broke that fellowship. As a result, sin separated man from God, and man had to leave the Garden.

"How then would God ever mend the rift? By sending his 'Son' Jesus, the Christ. The profound mystery is that Jesus was not merely human, but deity incarnate—God himself in the flesh. God became like us so that we could somehow become like him.

"But sin required a sacrifice, and it was Jesus' sacrificial death on the cross that became the atonement for our sin. When man obeys the gospel and accepts that unmerited gift of God's grace, then he is once again reconciled with God."

Richard took a deep breath and let it out slowly. "So much for Christian theology in a nutshell," said Richard, aware that he could have spent hours filling in the blanks.

Amy always admired the way Richard could reduce complex ideas to simple explanations that everyone could easily grasp.

"The next major theology is pretty much an oxymoron, since it denies that there *is* a 'theos,' or God. It's humanism. Humanism is all that talk about God being dead. In humanism there is no God. Man in his resplendent glory is all there is. Man is the crowning achievement of evolution's upward spiral.

"Of course, since man is nothing more than a highly evolved animal, there's no need worrying about either resurrection or reincarnation. When you die, you're dead all over like little dog Rover!

"For humanists, the best part is not having to run around worrying about how to be reconciled to some God. There simply *is* no God. Case closed, let's all go home.

"But the humanists have a real problem—in fact, a couple of problems. First, hardly anyone is truly willing to accept that there is no God. As they say, there aren't any atheists in foxholes—nor, I might add, in hospital waiting rooms or even electric chairs.

"And the second problem is that virtually everybody *wants* an afterlife. How else do you explain the Egyptian pyramids, the Indians' happy hunting ground, and the terra-cotta warriors in China?

"So humanism can never succeed. It bears within itself the seeds of its own destruction. And that is where New Age comes to its rescue—and also why it is so dangerous. It maintains the supremacy of the human being (consider, for example, all the New Age talk about 'human potential'), but provides both a God and an afterlife explanation, which of course is reincarnation.

"As for God, God is not dead, as the humanists say. No, in New Age, you and I *are* God! Or at least we *could be*, if only we could bring ourselves to realize it. And as for sin, the only 'sin' around is our metaphysical ignorance about who we really are.

"Right there, of course, is where they line up with Jesus for a photo opportunity. Jesus, so they say, was an ordinary human being like the rest of us until he realized his divinity. As the most highly evolved spiritual being ever to live on the earth, he became sufficiently enlightened to understand that he was God. In that understanding he was 'sinless.' He had overcome all ignorance about his true self."

Eric couldn't hold back any longer. "Isn't that the same man-realizes-himself-to-be-God theme that was so blasphemous about the controversial movie 'The Last Temptation of Christ'?"

"Precisely! Forget the adulterous dream sequence that all the Christians were protesting. The movie's sinister message, just as in New Age teaching, is that Jesus was no different from any of the rest of us. And if *we* would only say that we are God, like Jesus did, then we too would have what Jesus had, which is—are you ready for this?—"

"Christ consciousness!" Sara interjected.

"Bingo! It must be ESP!" Richard smiled.

"And, catch this," he said, turning serious again. "When we finally acknowledge that we are God, then we have *at-one-ment* with ourselves! Like Christ, we become our own Savior!"

Eric's mind was running a mile a minute. "*At-one-ment*? What a cheap substitute for the precious blood of Jesus which became our *atonement*!"

"In New Age, Eric, I'm afraid that hyphens are always agents of 'cheap.' Take the New Agers' manipulated use of 'dis-ease,' for example. The only reason you have cancer is because you are *not at ease* with yourself!"

"I'll tell you one thing," Eric replied wryly. "If truth can be so easily hyphenated, then I sure don't want to be around on Judgment Day when their Easternized beliefs are finally dis-**oriented** and their demonic perversion forever dis-**possessed**!"

Richard and Sara rolled their eyes at each other!

For Amy, the discussion brought to mind a passage from the Bible that had always disturbed her. "Didn't Jesus say something about all of us being God, like he was God?"

"That's not exactly it," said Richard, "but you're close. It comes from John chapter 10, where the Jews are accusing Jesus of blasphemy for claiming to be God. Jesus gave an intriguing response: 'Is it not written in your Law, "I have said you are gods"?'

"New Agers love this passage! What they fail to appreciate, of course, is the context of both the immediate passage, and, even more so, the Old Testament text from which it is taken.

"In John 10 Jesus is quoting from Psalm 82:6, which is referring to the unjust judges of Israel— almost derisively—as gods, with a little 'g.' What New Agers never go on to tell you is the rest of the story. Far from these unjust judges being immortal gods, the God of all creation who *is* immortal says to them in anger: 'I said, "You are 'gods' . . . but you will die like mere men."'"

Richard the teddy bear became Richard the lion-hearted: "I tell you, the blasphemy wrapped up in the idea of 'Christ consciousness' ought to make New Agers bolt their doors in terror against the inevitable appearance of the Grim Reaper. Let them call it *karma* if they wish. Either way, there's going to be *literal* hell to pay for setting ourselves up in the place of God!"

Hebrews 9:27 flashed into Sara's mind. "I'm beginning to see why you wanted us to remember Hebrews 9:27. It's a double-barreled warning, isn't it? Dying *once*, and then facing *judgment*."

"You're absolutely right, Sara. And why do I get the distinct feeling that New Agers want to replace the first part of the verse with reincarnation in the vain hope that somehow, someway, they can avoid the second part—*judgment*?"

"What a lethal cocktail you get," Sara said, thinking aloud, "when you try to mix New Age teaching with biblical Christianity."

The four of them sat silently, soaking in the enormous eternal implications of the spiritual warfare that was so succinctly summarized in the blasphemous notion of "Christ consciousness."

14

◆

In Sweet
Fellowship

The coffee was fresh-brewed, and Amy's prune cake with the caramel icing was surprisingly delicious. "Surprisingly" was the exact word Eric had heard coming out of his mouth when complimenting Amy, undoubtedly because he had mentally recoiled when Amy announced the dessert of the day. "*Prune* cake?" Eric had wondered. "Does she think we're ready for a *retirement home*?" Now he was literally eating his words and thoroughly enjoying it.

"This icing is absolutely divine!" Sara exclaimed with delight. Amy beamed, luxuriating in the praise for her culinary skills.

Richard was just finishing his last bite and joined in the accolade: "Ummm, *great*! It doesn't get any better than this!" He pushed his chair back from the table and reached for his coffee. After a sip, Richard let it be known that he wanted no detail left uncovered: "So, is there anything you haven't told us about Shirley's seminar?"

As it turned out, Eric had purposely saved the best for last. They still hadn't talked about the visualization sequence which he and Sara had found so fascinating. Trying to remember every word—and imitating Shirley as much as possible—Eric recounted the outer-space flight of fancy that had ended up back on earth at the foot of the tree in the middle of the garden.

When Eric mentioned how struck he had been at the similarity between Shirley's visualization exercise and the Garden of Eden, Richard could not help but pull Eric's leg. "You do know, don't you, that the Bible says Shirley MacLaine was in the Garden of Eden?"

Eric realized that Richard was trying to draw him into something foolish, so he played along. "Oh, really?"

"Yeah. It's in Genesis chapter 3, where the serpent said (and here Richard made a play on the word *surely*), 'Shirley, you will not die!'"

Sara laughed so hard that she thought *she* would surely die! Eric chuckled appreciatively. He had heard lots of Shirley MacLaine jokes, but never that one. Yet when he regained his seriousness, the joke reminded him of the other part of that same passage, where the serpent had implied to Eve that she too could be God if only she would eat of the forbidden fruit.

"It's absolutely scary what a parallel there is. In the Garden, the serpent delivered to Eve the exact same one-two punch being delivered by New Agers: 1) Because of reincarnation, you will never die; and 2) if you only choose it to be so, then you too can be God!"

The others all nodded in solemn agreement.

"So what did you see when Shirley introduced you to your higher self?" Amy asked curiously.

"You're not going to believe this," said Eric, "but at that very moment—I can't explain why—the first thing that came to my mind was a loaf of Wonder Bread!"

Richard had a field day with all the cosmic possibilities suggested by the Wonder Bread. "Does that mean that you're going to make a lot of *dough*? Or simply that your higher self is extremely well *bred*? Perhaps the Akashic Records know how much your lower self likes to *loaf*!"

"Enough! Enough!" Eric begged, as Amy shook her head in mock embarrassment. "If you think that's weird, you haven't heard anything yet. Tell them what *you* saw, Sara."

"Well, you're not going to believe this," said Sara, "but when Shirley introduced us to our higher selves, I kept visualizing a foot-long *hot dog*!"

Amy gave Richard that look that unmistakably said: "Don't start!"

Relieved at having been spared all the possible hot dog puns, Sara did confess Eric's own earlier dubious connection. "On the way home, Eric and I were talking about what we saw, and we couldn't help but speculate about the cosmic meaning of the combination between hot dogs and Wonder Bread. Eric was sure it meant that we were once soul mates!"

"I thought I detected something cosmic between you two," Amy said with a smile.

"The problem, we decided," said Eric seriously,

"was that one's higher self could be anything that pops into the mind. As we were leaving the building, we heard two or three people saying that what they saw at the foot of the tree was Jesus Christ. Of course, that's not surprising, since Shirley associated the higher self with prayer, and with the one who answers prayers."

Richard immediately spotted the danger. "Praise God that some of them saw Jesus, but what an incredible risk to be taking. Instead of our being made 'in the image of God,' as the Bible says, God ends up being made in our own **image**-ination. Given the creativity of one's imagination, God could be anything from Jesus Christ to hot dogs and Wonder Bread!"

Sara shared her own speculation: "I have a feeling that Eric and I were just hungry about the time we did the visualization bit."

"You may be right," Richard responded with a smile, "but in all seriousness I think you've hit on yet another danger: When people are *spiritually* hungry, they're willing to accept almost anything that might give them a sense of the divine. At that point it's all too easy for Satan to send them a dizzying delusion of self-godhood."

Eric agreed. "If spiritual fraud can sometimes *fill* a temporary need, it can never permanently *fulfill* our deepest longings."

Sara could only echo that thought. "I can remember the excitement I felt when Tina first introduced me to the New Age. It was so full of promise, but in the end it left me empty and confused. Now that I've renewed my faith in Christ and submitted my life to his leading, I have a genuine peace that I find completely fulfilling."

———— ◆ ————

Throughout his study of the constellation of beliefs and practices known as New Age, Richard had given a lot of thought as to why people so energetically launch themselves into that unlikely orbit. Among the many people he had counseled out of New Age were a large number of former Roman Catholics. They had talked about their heavy sense of guilt, coming from school days when the sisters had mercilessly driven visions of punishing hellfire into their impressionable minds. For many Catholics, the Church symbolized a monolithic, overbearing institution that authoritatively imposed limitless, seemingly arbitrary rules.

Richard began explaining some of this background. "It isn't just my counselees," Richard noted. "In many of the New Age books I've read, I have noticed a tremendous undercurrent of resentment against Christianity always viewed through the eyes of 'the church.'"

"You're right," Eric agreed. "Sometimes in my own reading I wanted to scream in outrage at organized religion for having hidden the simple message of Christ in elaborate ecclesiastical trappings."

"No wonder the world finds 'Christianity' to be unappealing," Amy observed. "From what you say, it looks like the church itself is driving a lot of people into the waiting arms of the New Age!"

"And it isn't just Catholics," Richard continued. "Many of the people turning to New Age have come out of mainline Protestant denominations. I can't begin to tell you how many people have told me of their midlife crises and of their frantic search for meaning. They've graduated from college, worked hard climbing the corporate ladder, and accumulated every adult toy they could think of to make them happy, but ended up in their late forties unhappy, divorced, and struggling with teenagers on drugs.

"Many of these people followed their instincts and went back to the churches where they had grown up. They knew their materialistic lives were in desperate need of a spiritual component. But what they discovered in the churches was just more materialism: big buildings, big parking lots, big budgets, big attendance. Size and prosperity were obviously considered signs of church success—just like success in the secular world. And with that startling disillusionment, another bunch of lost souls woke up the next day in the disguised spiritual embrace of New Age."

"The sad irony," said Eric, "is that the New Age promised these folks a more enlightened spiritualism, but ended up in the same materialistic ditch, taking their money with as much fervor as any charlatan evangelist. Do you all realize how much money we've spent on New Age books alone? Not to mention what Sara spent on Tina, what both of us spent on Kevin Peterson, and how much Shirley MacLaine charged for introducing us to our higher selves. New Age is one of the most successful growth industries in America!"

"I wish it were just a matter of money," Richard noted, "because that would make it so much easier to expose. The problem is that New Age can actually meet some deeply felt needs. For instance, as strange as it may seem, many of my counselees are Jewish. New Age has captured the attention of many Jews because the notion of reincarnation gives them hope for an afterlife. Historically, Jews have never had a great afterlife theology, and most cultural Jews today doubt whether there is any life beyond the grave.

"Even better," said Richard, "New Age allows Jews to accept Jesus as a great teacher and master, without ever having to become a Christian. It's hard for most of us to understand, but the decision for a Jew to become a Christian is as much a cultural conversion as a faith conversion."

Amy had heard Richard talking about his conversations with Jewish New Agers, but had never considered that particular difficulty. "Isn't it sad," she said, genuinely moved, "that so many people get caught up in New Age only because they are running away from something else that has failed to fulfill them? Worse yet, it's often some form of Christianity that leaves them empty!"

———— ◆ ————

For Sara the emptiness and searching had been all too real—on *both* sides of her encounter with New Age. Like so many others, she had turned to New Age in the first place because of a vacuum in her own life; but after tasting of psychics and gurus, she had been left emptier still. Amy's observation prompted Sara to share something that had been on her mind throughout the meal.

"Can I tell you something from my own experience? Over the last several weeks I've come to

realize that one of the main reasons for my emptiness in the New Age was a lack of anything like
Christian fellowship. In the New Age you're on
your own. There is no concept like church, or a
spiritual family, or fellowship. You find yourself in
virtual isolation, floating from one guru or seminar
to another.

"In a way I guess it's the down side of a belief
system centering on Self. In New Age it's all Self,
with little room for others. But Self without others is
not a happy existence.

"I have to admit that Christian fellowship itself is
not always what it should be. I remember how difficult it was to talk to my Christian friends where I
used to attend church. They were *social* but not very
spiritual. That too was a kind of emptiness. But
having now discovered a church filled with people
who really know God and the Bible, I've found
Christians who know what it means to be a *family* of
God. Good families truly fill needs, don't they?

"And speaking of *family*, I can't begin to tell you
how comfortable I am being in your home today,
and just knowing the two of you. It's obvious that
what you have in your personal lives and in your
marriage is something special that only a well-
grounded faith in Christ could give you. Unlike
those whom I met in New Age circles, I don't sense
any restlessness or frantic searching.

"Nor is there any game-playing with soul mates
and signs of the zodiac—just pure, genuine, godly
love. The love that you have is what I was searching
for when I got sidetracked into New Age. Now I can
see that what makes both of you so special is the love

of Christ living in you. And that is what I want in my own life.

"How can I ever thank you enough for opening your hearts and sharing his love with me?"

Eric was touched by Sara's sincere affirmation of faith. How could he have been so blessed as to have her in his life? He reached over and took her hand, squeezing it gently.

In the mood of the moment, Richard followed suit with Amy.

It was a precious time of shared Christian love. All around the table there were tears of joy.

15

◆

Going Mainstream

The summer was over and Eric was back in classes for the fall semester of his third and final year. He and Sara were formally dating now, although his studies and part-time clerking kept him busier than ever. Eric loved to remind Sara that "the law is a jealous mistress!" Never one to be outdone, Sara had responded, "Just see if your jealous mistress will give you a good-night kiss!"

Their most precious time together was sharing worship on Sundays and the fellowship they enjoyed at the Wednesday night Bible study for law students, held in the home of Robert Johnson, one of Eric's professors. Prof. Johnson and most of the students were members of the Christian Legal Society, and naturally Eric reveled in that association.

Prof. Johnson had encouraged Eric to enroll in his Law and Morality Seminar, and Eric was glad he had done so. It was a break from tough lecture courses like Tax, Constitutional Law, and Corporations. And, more importantly, it was a *paper* course.

That meant no final exam! Just a couple weeks of hard labor cranking out a 25-page paper on some subject involving both legal and moral issues, and Eric would be home free.

For his topic, Eric chose the hot-button issue of gay rights. But he wasn't altogether sure about the title that first came to mind: "Is God Gay?" Eric didn't know if Prof. Johnson's normally gracious sense of humor would stretch quite that far!

The seminar met for two hours each Tuesday afternoon. There was no agenda apart from some outside reading which Prof. Johnson assigned. The professor would throw out a hard question, and within minutes the discussion would head off in all sorts of interesting directions. And, of course, it was always the lions versus the Christians.

Eric and two or three other active, Bible-believing Christians were usually pitted against six or seven political radicals who regarded themselves as everything from atheists to Marxists. (Eric wasn't fooled. The "Marxists" would actually be "Communists" but for the fact that Communism is no longer politically correct even for Marxists!) The remainder of the 24 students were a mixed bag in their religious orientation.

———— ◆ ————

"Today," Prof. Johnson began, "I want us to think about the question 'What is morality?' How do we define it? Where does it come from? How does it differ, if at all, from ethics or law?"

The answers were in some way predictable. The

Christian students defined morality as the standards that God set forth in the Bible for right conduct. "So what if I took away your Christian Bible?" Prof. Johnson pressed. "Would there be any basis for morality apart from revealed Scripture?"

One of the Christian students, anxious to defend God's revelation, said "no." But Eric reckoned that there was a moral order in the world brought about by God's creative power, wholly apart from revelation. "The Bible specifically articulates morality in a way that cannot be found elsewhere," he said, "but God created man with moral consciousness and appeals to that conscience even when a person is unaware of the Bible."

Eric pulled out his Bible and read from Romans chapter 2, beginning at verse 14:

> Indeed, when Gentiles, who do not have the law, do by nature things required by the law, they are a law for themselves, even though they do not have the law, since they show that the requirements of the law are written on their hearts, their consciences also bearing witness, and their thoughts now accusing, now even defending them.

That set Bill off! Bill was one of those often-wrong-but-never-in-doubt agnostics who couldn't stand Bible-thumping Christians. "There you go! You read from the Bible in order to prove that something exists apart from the Bible!"

"Okay," Eric conceded, "but regardless of the source, the principle is still true. Wherever you look, in whatever time, in whatever culture, there are some things that *everybody* recognizes as right, and other things that *everybody* recognizes as wrong. And *that* is morality."

"Poppycock!" Bill retorted. "There is nothing that *everybody* finds either right or wrong. Take, for example, the African tribes who practice wife-swapping. Or head-hunting cannibals. Or a Greek society that openly condoned homosexuality. Or infanticide by exposure, practiced both by the ancient Romans and today's Chinese."

"But those practices are *perversions* of moral law which the vast majority of people throughout time have condemned as immoral," Eric urged. "The very fact that you cite those specific examples is proof that such practices are not within the moral norms that one might expect."

At that point Prof. Johnson intervened. "Is there anything that might be called 'universal morality'?" From the students' reaction, the class was about evenly split on the question.

Claire, a self-proclaimed feminist, insisted that there could be no such thing as *universal* morality as long as there were *any* exceptions. Besides, she asserted, "morality has always been male oriented. Morality is power, and power is masculine." For Claire, that was that!

"Let me reword the question," said the professor. "Is there no such thing as absolute right and wrong?"

"No," said Bill, "absolutely not!"

Eric loved that ironic response. "*Absolutely* not?" he chided.

"Okay, then *definitely* not," said Bill, somewhat embarrassed.

First one student then another agreed. "How can there be absolute right and wrong," asked one student, "when not even *we* can agree on the definition of morality?"

Another student seconded that sentiment. "If there was such a thing as absolute right and wrong, we wouldn't be having our civil wars over such issues as gay rights and abortion. Everyone would agree."

Cathy, one of the Christian students, couldn't stand it any longer. "Does that mean that, if someone decides to take your car, it's not immoral? After all, by taking it they obviously don't think you have a right to have it. And by your definition of morality, since you don't agree about who has the right of possession it's not immoral."

That brought Bill to his emotional feet! "What a bunch of rubbish! *Of course* in our society theft is considered immoral, but that's *our society*! In other societies, property is not viewed in the same way. What's immoral for us may not be immoral for someone else."

Eric prodded Bill: "In what society is theft *not* viewed as immoral?"

Bill was momentarily caught short. "Well, wherever property is held in common for the good of all society," he murmured weakly.

Again the professor broke in. "It seems some of you are suggesting that moral right and wrong is relative—that it is determined by each society, and therefore is neither absolute nor universal. Is that true?"

A large number of the students nodded in agreement.

"Does that mean there is no such thing as inherent evil?"

Again most of the heads nodded in the affirmative.

"Then let me just ask you this," Prof. Johnson said with a dramatic pause, "what about the Holocaust? Was it not inherently evil?"

Eric could tell that Prof. Johnson had carefully chosen his punch line. Who could possibly deny that the Holocaust was inherently evil? But to his amazement, the more liberal students stuck to their guns. "No," "No," "No," came the responses one after another.

"Are you kidding me?" Eric fairly shouted to himself. "But what else could they have said?" Eric thought. "Once you commit yourself to a position that denies absolute morality, all you have left is relative morality. And when all you have is relative morality, then—they're right—nothing could be inherently evil!"

Eric thought he would stop this nonsense in its tracks by appealing to one of the three Jewish students in the class. Turning to Brian Lieberman, Eric put the obvious question: "As a Jew, Brian, how do you regard the Holocaust? Surely *you* believe it was inherently evil!"

Eric was not prepared for the answer. "I know what you're thinking, Eric, but—no—I don't think that the Holocaust was *inherently* evil. Naturally, as a Jew, I hate the thought that I might be killed merely because I am a Jew, and I sure wouldn't want it happening to my family or any other Jew for that matter. But I can't impose my morality on anyone else."

Eric's jaw dropped. "That's unbelievable!" he groaned. "Have we really proceeded that far with all the nonjudgmental silliness floating around?"

Remarkably, Brian wasn't the only Jewish student on this wavelength. Jonathan Greenfield jumped in to suggest that, since the Nazis made it official policy to exterminate Jews, that alone was proof that, in their minds, they did not consider genocide immoral.

Eric was completely dismayed. "Are you telling me that a society can simply choose what is right and wrong *for them*?"

"Haven't they always?" Jonathan asked, nonplussed.

"Sure, but it doesn't mean they have chosen correctly or morally," Eric pleaded. "Otherwise, what right did we have to punish Nazi war crimes in the Nuremberg Trials?"

"As conquerors," Jonathan offered, "we had the right to exercise our power over Germany."

"So might makes right?" Eric pressed.

"Yes. Or social contract. Or pragmatism. C'mon, Eric, don't be so self-righteous. Did you see the movie 'Alive'? The survivors of the plane crash became their own little society. Under the necessity of circumstances, what had been *wrong*—eating human flesh—became *right*!"

Eric almost steamed at that analogy. "But in 'Alive' we're talking about a clearly exceptional situation, not some coolly deliberated governmental policy of genocide!"

Neither Jonathan nor Brian seemed to have the heart to further defend their position. In fact, the air of certainty in the words they spoke was betrayed by their uncomfortable body language.

Prof. Johnson apparently had heard these arguments before. He calmly observed that when a person takes a philosophical position of any stance, the only way to test the validity of his position is to extend the position to its logical extreme. If it works in the extreme case, then it is likely to be valid under all normal circumstances. And, more importantly, he pointed out—vice versa. If one's position does *not* work in the extreme, then it is not likely to be valid at all.

On the strength of that observation, Prof. Johnson cautioned the students that if they were determined to believe in relative morality, then they would have to live with the obvious problem of a Holocaust that was not inherently evil. "Can you really live with that conclusion?" he asked, knowing that they probably couldn't.

Two hours had breezed by unnoticed, and there was still no agreement on even the basic definition of morality. But what Eric was hearing from his fellow students was alarming, to say the least. Eric left the room a wiser, but sadder, man.

——— ◆ ———

"You just wouldn't have believed it," Eric said to Sara over dinner that night. "Here were the future guardians of law and order saying that nothing is absolute, and that right and wrong are relative.

"I guarantee you that they're not going to buy this nonsense when they are 'on duty' in court dealing with crimes such as robbery, rape, and murder.

They know full well that acts like those are immoral as well as illegal. So how can they so easily walk out of the courtroom and blithely abandon the idea of absolutes in their personal lives? It's sheer moral schizophrenia!"

"What gets me," said a mystified Sara, "are the Jewish guys. Did they really say that the Holocaust was not inherently evil?"

"Actually, I feel sorry for them," mused Eric. "I'll bet you that on their way home tonight they were asking themselves the very same question.

"The problem is that they've all come up through a value-neutral educational system which has indoctrinated them, first, in relative morality, and, second, in being nonjudgmental because everything's relative. They were just repeating the party line and had never before been forced to carry that line to its logical extreme."

Sara offered a clarification. "From what you're telling me, it looks like value-neutral education is not so neutral after all. When you neutralize values, it doesn't mean that you have *no* values. If the Holocaust is any indication, it means you end up with *horrendous* values!"

"I tell you, Sara, I think there is a generational and cultural shift going on around us, not terribly different from the New Age movement itself.

"On my way over to pick you up, I got to thinking back on what Shirley MacLaine and the other New Agers were saying when they talked about monism. Remember? All is one, so there is no difference between good and evil, or right and wrong. That's exactly what these guys were saying today. And it wasn't just Bill and the radicals. It was the prevailing sentiment."

"And what they said about the Nazis *choosing* what was right for them also sounds pretty New Agey," Sara noted. "In fact, do you remember when we came across more than one New Age author suggesting that the *Jews themselves* actually chose their extermination? Frightening thought, isn't it?"

Eric got to thinking further about the parallels between the New Age movement and what he had been hearing in the Law and Morality Seminar. It occurred to him that New Age thought had apparently filtered down in another way as well.

"Sara, do you recall what I was telling you about the Bengal tigers hypothetical that Prof. Johnson gave us a couple of weeks ago?"

Eric was referring to one of the first sessions, in which Prof. Johnson had asked the class to list all the human rights on one side of the blackboard and all the so-called animal rights on the other side. When "right to life" appeared on both sides of the board, the professor asked if it was the same "right to life" for animals as for man.

A large number of students responded in the affirmative, so Prof. Johnson offered a hypothetical: "Suppose you have the option of saving, on one hand, an innocent human being; or, on the other hand, the last 500 Bengal tigers on the planet. Which would you choose to save?"

To Eric's surprise, 11 students had chosen the tigers. Even when Prof. Johnson changed the hypo so that there was no extinction of the tigers involved, six students had still chosen the tigers over the innocent human being.

"What I didn't tell you," Eric said to Sara, "was that Prof. Johnson got the weirdest explanation from Sam Bates as to why he would save the tigers. I'll never forget Sam's words. He said, 'You're right, professor. In an abstract sense, a human being is more valuable than an animal. But when you take the lesser energy value of an animal and multiply it by 500, it amounts to something greater than the energy value of a single human being.'"

"*Energy value?*" Sara asked quizzically.

"Does that sound familiar?" Eric asked.

"Are you thinking about the New Age explanation for God, that he—or it—was God Force, or *energy?*"

"Exactly!" said Eric. "Regardless of all the talk about 'souls' and 'soul mates' in New Age philosophy, their idea of 'souls' is not anywhere close to the biblical view. For New Agers, the soul is nothing but energy. And when you combine that with the belief that 'all is one,' what you come up with is animals and man being made of the same energy, separated only by some *quantity* of energy."

Sara was already racing ahead. "No wonder there is so little regard among New Agers for the sanctity of life, whether it be abortion, infanticide, euthanasia, or even murder, according to that Ramtha character. 'Energy value' is light-years away from sanctity of life!"

"And, stupid me, I thought that New Age was alive and well only in Looneyville!" Eric lamented. "Now I find it at my own doorstep in the legal profession. Wow, it's not just psychics, astral projections, and reincarnation anymore. They're all just window dressing. New Age morality is now mainstream America!"

"Welcome to the new world order, counselor," Sara said ominously.

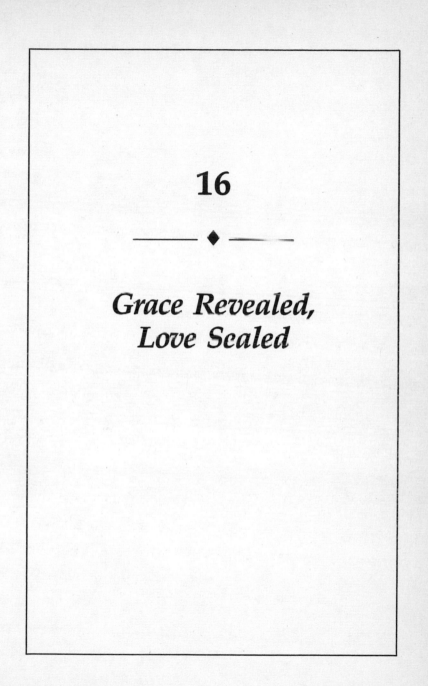

16

◆

Grace Revealed,
Love Sealed

The silver-white beach stretched out for miles ahead of them, with the surging waves advancing relentlessly onto the shore. As the foaming water receded in broad overlapping sheets into the vast ocean reservoir, Eric's eyes quickly scanned for treasures left behind on the sand. Seashells were the ocean's gift to those who would come out and "shake hands" with it.

Quick. Over there. A momentary glint of light seems to be reflected off a tiny bit of crustacean. Run, before the oncoming tide sweeps it away, never to be seen again. Eric dashed into the shallow foam just in time to retrieve a perfectly formed sand dollar.

"Look what I've found, Sara."

"Oh, it's lovely!"

"It's for you, my love," said Eric romantically, as he carefully handed the prize to Sara. "One perfect treasure for another."

Sara melted into Eric's arms.

—— ◆ ——

In a sheltered cove a mile or so up the beach, they sat on the sand with their backs against lava-like rocks that jutted out from the land and ended fingerlike at the water's edge. For a while they sat in shared silence, mesmerized by the sound of the waves. Sara reminisced over the months since she had first met Eric, and on the unlikely events which had brought them together: Tina and her healing crystals, the Bodhi Tree bookstore, Kevin Peterson's dream seminar and "Tom" his pretended Irish pickpocket.

How, Sara wondered, could she ever have gotten so desperate about her love life as to have been sucked into the vortex of psychic phenomenon, and possibly even into the forbidden realm of demons? By what great mercy had God rescued her from a spiritual odyssey that so easily could have been disastrous, both now and for eternity!

And what of the special man of God sitting next to her? How could she ever be sufficiently thankful to God for sending such a spiritual man into her life— to restore her trust in men, to open her eyes to the truth, to love her as she had never been loved before: purely, deeply, completely.

Eric, too, was thinking back over those almost saga-like months. Whoever would have guessed, he mused silently, that the lowly sophomore with the wicked sense of humor just a couple of seats down the row in English Lit would one day become the object of his deepest affection. "Isn't it funny how God works in our lives?" he thought.

Eric could hardly grasp the feelings he had for Sara. Far more than even a lawyer's glib tongue could ever express, he loved her dearly. He loved her quick wit and ready laughter; her seriousness, yet her wonderful lightheartedness; her virtue! Most of all, he loved her innocence and vulnerability and honesty of heart.

In the honesty of his own heart, Eric felt that Sara was the one with greater strength. If *he* had taught *her* something of Scripture and true peace in Christ, *she* had taught *him* the importance of intellectual integrity and of admitting when you are wrong. Sara, thought Eric, was first and foremost a woman of enormous courage. How he treasured her spiritual fortitude! With her at his side, surely he could never fail to be a man of strength for her in return.

Eric's thoughts turned to the incredible way in which he and Sara had found each other. Given all the talk about reincarnation, he was struck with the irony: It was as if they had known each other in two different lifetimes. The first, in school, had been as distant acquaintances. The second had entwined their very souls!

—— ◆ ——

Eric was the first to break the silence. "You know, Sara, when you look at the waves coming in, over and over again, you can see why reincarnation has such appeal to so many people. All throughout nature, there are cycles and instances of repetition. Here on the beach, the waves pound against the shore with thunderous crashes, then subside gently and sweep out to sea, only to come roaring back once again.

"The seasons, too, come and go, only to reappear. The birds over there migrate great distances, only to find their way back home year after year.

"I was just thinking a moment ago," said Eric as he turned to look at Sara, "that, in a way, even you and I have had two lives. The first was in our student days, when we saw each other only from afar. And now, reborn, as it were, we're sharing our love together."

Reincarnation-like though it was, Sara almost swooned at the lovely picture that Eric's analogy had painted. "I've thought about life's many cycles too, and I think you're right. The idea of reincarnation *can* give hope to a person who longs for it. On its face, reincarnation speaks of second chances and renewal, and of a time to start all over again.

"But when I was thinking about the waves awhile ago, I sensed a different, even more powerful image. It was of God's grace. I got to thinking how many times I've messed up in my life and let God down. But each time I fail him, he seeks me out relentlessly with wave after wave of mercy to wipe clean whatever doubt and sinful debris I've left about.

"It makes me think of that song we sing at the Bible study:

The steadfast love of the Lord never ceases;
His mercies never come to an end; They are
new every morning, new every morning;
Great is thy faithfulness!

"Over the past few months I've come to realize like never before that God's grace is his moment-by-moment love in my life. It seeks me out ceaselessly, wave after renewing wave."

Eric loved that image. "And that's why reincarnation finishes a distant second to faith in Christ, despite whatever hope the idea of many different lifetimes may seem to offer. Reincarnation promises a second chance, but can never completely clean the slate. It simply reintroduces over and over again the same problem of human fallibility from which we can never, on our own, truly escape.

"No wonder," Eric thought aloud, "that Buddha himself referred to reincarnation as 'that infernal wheel.' Those were not words of fondness! In fact, his so-called 'steps to enlightenment' were intended not to help people *stay on* the wheel of reincarnation but to somehow *get off it!*"

What he said triggered Sara's mind. "Maybe *that's* the true interpretation of my dream!" she speculated half-seriously. "The ferris wheel may have been pointing me to the futility of putting my faith in reincarnation. Regardless of whatever relationships come into our lives, there can be no peace as long as we are going 'round and 'round in endless spiritual circles!"

"I don't know if that's what was intended," Eric smiled, "but I'm sure the analogy fits.

"And I'll tell you what analogy fits even better," said Eric, suddenly noticing a butterfly on the breeze. "It's the ugly larva that is transformed into a beautiful butterfly. God's grace is superior to reincarnation because it doesn't merely *reinvent* a person, it *transforms* us."

"Ooh, I never thought of that," Sara said excitedly. "Butterflies are a great analogy!"

"When a person is in relationship with God through obedient faith in Christ," Eric continued, "death becomes the doorway to an afterlife that never brings one back again into a world of pain, suffering, and sorrow. It's not just another lifetime *here* that I want, but another kind of life altogether—like the butterfly."

As he thought further about it, Eric warmed to all the possible parallels. "The butterfly starts off as a wormlike caterpillar, then is transformed through a process of metamorphosis into a gossamer-winged butterfly. There's no returning time and time again into the body of a slug. Instead, a true change occurs in both form and function.

"What's neat about that," Eric gathered enthusiasm, "is that, in its new body, the butterfly has a completely transformed character. As long as it is a wormlike caterpillar, it is bent on destruction, eating everything in sight. But when it becomes a butterfly, it has no capacity to destroy, only to bring life and spread joy!"

Sara was delighted with that thought. "And you think that's what heaven will be like for us?"

"Exactly! It's not just harps and golden streets and pearly gates. We are going to be so radically transformed in heaven—with resplendent bodies fit for eternity—that we will be as different in form and function from who we are now as the butterfly is from the slug."

"The only thing I don't like about that," said Sara wistfully, "is that the Bible says there will be no . . ." Sara caught herself before finishing the sentence.

"You mean, no *marriage* in heaven?" Eric anticipated.

"Yeah. I know we will be like the angels, not needing human companionship; and I know that we will be completely fulfilled in the presence of God forever; but I wouldn't want to think of no longer being married to the one I love."

Sara was a little nervous bringing up the "M" word. She and Eric had spoken of love, but never specifically about marriage.

Eric didn't seem to mind the topic of conversation. In fact, he reached for Sara's hand and said, "It only says there won't be *marriage* as we know it. It doesn't say that we won't consciously be together."

Sara's mind raced. Was Eric using the word "we" broadly—as for all of God's children—or did he mean . . . ?

Before she could think further, Eric was tying his comment back into what Sara had said before about grace. "What makes a spiritual metamorphosis like that possible is God's grace. Unlike reincarnation, God's grace brings about a transformation in our lives that begins even now, *before* we die.

"Through faith and submission to Christ," he went on, "there is a spiritual change that takes place within every believer. That's what Jesus was telling Nicodemus when he talked about being 'born again': Born again *spiritually*, never to die again in an earthly body."

"My favorite verse, John 3:16, comes right after that," Sara said: "For God so loved the world that he gave his one and only Son, that whoever believes in him shall not perish but have eternal life."

Eric admired the diligence with which Sara had been studying her Bible. It occurred to him that even that was a kind of transformation.

Yet he could not help but share with her the most sublime transformation of all time. "Just think, Sara. God's grace comes to us through Christ, who —as the Son of God—experienced the most incredible metamorphosis ever to have occurred: God became man and lived among us so that we could be transformed by his grace into glory!"

"That thought sends chills down my spine," said Sara.

"If that gives you chills," Eric built up into a crescendo, "how about this passage that I first memorized when I was just a kid:

> Who shall separate us from the love of Christ? Shall trouble or hardship or persecution or famine or nakedness or danger or sword? As it is written: 'For your sake we face death all day long; we are considered as sheep to be slaughtered.'
>
> No, in all these things we are more than conquerors through him who loved us. For I am convinced that neither death nor life, neither angels nor demons, neither the present nor the future, nor any powers, neither height nor depth, nor anything else in all creation, will be able to separate us from the love of God that is in Christ Jesus our Lord (Romans 8:35-39)."

"What a promise!" Sara exclaimed. "Who could have experienced his forgiving love more than me? Who could have *needed* his love more than me!"

"You're not unique in that regard," Eric responded. "I don't know of *anyone* who hasn't cried out for God's love and mercy—not even New Agers, whether they know it or not. What they are searching for is indeed 'cosmic'—as in the God who rules over life and death; over angels and demons; over the past, the present, and the future. What could be more captivating than the Lord of the universe loving us with inseparable love—a love well within our grasp in this one lifetime!

"If only all of us could surrender the self-defeating notion of *being* God, or *acting* as if we are God, and discover instead the exaltation which comes with humbly accepting God's grace! What could be more 'cosmic' than having the God of all creation as your friend! What could be more transforming than knowing you have his love!"

Sara rested her head on Eric's shoulder. She was sure he was right. Nothing could be more transforming than knowing that you are loved!

——— ◆ ———

"I sure enjoyed our time at the beach last week," Sara said, the dancing candlelight playing softly on her cheek.

"It *was* wonderful, wasn't it?" said Eric, caressing Sara with a look of love.

"And thank you for tonight. It's been absolutely glorious!" Sara sat back from the table as the waiter reached over to remove the plates and serving dishes. "The food was delicious. Absolutely delicious," she said again for emphasis. "When you told me to be sure and dress up, I had no idea what an elegant evening you had in mind."

Eric was ecstatic that Sara was enjoying the moment. "A guy has to surprise the woman he loves every now and then, doesn't he?"

"The woman he loves every now and then?" Sara tested him playfully.

"You know what I mean!" Eric said, smiling at Sara's searching distinction. "To *surprise* her every now and then."

"Well, you outdid yourself tonight!"

The waiter reappeared and reeled off the tempting desserts available.

"I don't think I could eat another bite," Sara said, thoroughly satisfied.

"Oh, sure you could," Eric insisted. "At least split something with me."

"Okay, I'll have a bite of whatever you're having."

"Great. How about . . . uh . . . the crème gateaux? And coffee?"

"You're on."

Eric tried not to seem too distracted as the waiter left the table. But he was on the edge of his seat with anticipation. Within moments he could see the waiter making his way from the far side of the restaurant toward their table.

Sara had not noticed what would not have been a surprise to Eric—that during the evening all the other tables around them had almost magically emptied. Eric and Sara were alone in the corner of the restaurant.

"I believe these are for you, madam," said the waiter with a regal formality. He held out a long white box wrapped in red ribbon with a wide figure-eight bow on one end.

"For me?" Sara asked, taken totally aback. "Is this another one of your surprises?" A big smile flashed across Eric's face.

Sara quickly removed the ribbon and squealed with delight when she saw the dozen red roses nestled in the green tissue paper. "Counselor, are you trying to bribe the jury? They're beautiful!"

"I just want you to know how much I love you, Sara."

"And I love you, too," said Sara radiantly. "With all my heart."

Eric was absolutely bursting with affection. "So what do you think, Sara? Do you think we've come a long way from psychics and gurus and crystals?"

"They seem like ancient history now, don't they?" Sara mused. "I promise you one thing, I'll never be caught off guard by crystals again."

"I'm not so sure about that," Eric said calculatedly, as he slipped his hand into his coat pocket. "I wonder if this particular crystal might not catch you off guard."

Eric opened a small black velvet box and turned it in Sara's direction. Inside, atop a yellow-gold band, was a sparkling diamond solitaire, dancing with color and brilliance in the flickering candlelight.

"Eric! It's . . . it's . . ." She could hardly finish the word "beautiful!" Eric took the ring from the box and carefully placed it on Sara's third finger, left hand.

"Sara, I can't begin to tell you how much I love you, and how much I want to be with you for the rest of my life."

Sara could hardly believe what she was hearing, but she knew she had to brace herself for what Eric would say next. It was a moment she had always dreamed of, and tried to imagine what it would be like. Could it really be happening? Was this the moment?

Eric paused and looked deeply into her eyes. "Sara, my love, will you marry me?" he asked with a relaxed smile.

Sara trembled at the words, but not at the thought. Even though Eric had indeed caught her off guard on this special evening, for weeks now Sara had seen it coming. Or at least she was *hoping* it would happen. Night after night she had fervently prayed that God would let her know if for any reason Eric was *not* to be the one. How then could she refuse?

She squeezed his hand hard. "Yes, of course I'll marry you," she said through teary eyes.

"And you don't mind that it's a crystal I'm giving you?" Eric teased.

"*This* crystal," said Sara, beaming, "is meant to be. It is a gift from God!"

"And so it is," Eric thought. "And so it is!"

Other Good
Harvest House Reading

**WHAT YOU NEED TO KNOW
ABOUT MASONS**
by *Ed Decker*

When Jeff Moore, a young Baptist minister, resigns from the Lodge, his family and his church relationships are thrown into chaos.

The hidden dangers of Freemasonry to the family and the church are fully communicated and the secret initiation ceremonies into the Lodge exposed in this creative approach to understanding one of the least-recognized cults in America.

**WHAT YOU NEED TO KNOW
ABOUT MORMONS**
by *Ed Decker*

In this informative book, the differences between Mormonism and Christianity are clearly presented. Through a series of conversations between neighbors, Decker presents the basic tenets of Mormonism and the countering truths of the Bible.

**WHAT YOU NEED TO KNOW ABOUT
JEHOVAH'S WITNESSES**
by *Lorri MacGregor*

One day in his devoted work for the Watch Tower Society, Joe Simpson finds himself on the doorstep of a concerned Christian who has learned how to talk to Jehovah's Witnesses. In the resulting conversations, the key elements of Jehovah's Witness doctrine are clearly and memorably refuted with Christian love and Scripture.

THE DAILY BIBLE
New International Version
Compiled by *F. LaGard Smith*

Unlike any other Bible you have ever read, *The Daily Bible* allows you to read the Scriptures chronologically as a powerful, uninterrupted account of God's interaction with human history.

You will see events from Creation through Revelation unfold before you like an epic novel, conveniently organized into 365 sections for daily reading. Gain a better overall perspective of Scripture by reading the Bible in the order the events occurred from the widely acclaimed New International Version.

Dear Reader:

We would appreciate hearing from you regarding this Harvest House book. It will enable us to continue to give you the best in Christian publishing.

1. What most influenced you to purchase *What You Need to Know About the New Age Movement*?
   - ☐ Author
   - ☐ Subject matter
   - ☐ Backcover copy
   - ☐ Recommendations
   - ☐ Cover/Title
   - ☐ _____

2. Where did you purchase this book?
   - ☐ Christian bookstore
   - ☐ General bookstore
   - ☐ Department store
   - ☐ Grocery store
   - ☐ Other

3. Your overall rating of this book:
   - ☐ Excellent ☐ Very good ☐ Good ☐ Fair ☐ Poor

4. How likely would you be to purchase other books by this author?
   - ☐ Very likely
   - ☐ Somewhat likely
   - ☐ Not very likely
   - ☐ Not at all

5. What types of books most interest you?
   (check all that apply)
   - ☐ Women's Books
   - ☐ Marriage Books
   - ☐ Current Issues
   - ☐ Self Help/Psychology
   - ☐ Bible Studies
   - ☐ Fiction
   - ☐ Biographies
   - ☐ Children's Books
   - ☐ Youth Books
   - ☐ Other _____

6. Please check the box next to your age group.
   - ☐ Under 18
   - ☐ 18-24
   - ☐ 25-34
   - ☐ 35-44
   - ☐ 45-54
   - ☐ 55 and over

Mail to: Editorial Director
Harvest House Publishers
1075 Arrowsmith
Eugene, OR 97402

Name _____

Address _____

City _____ State _____ Zip _____

**Thank you for helping us to help you
in future publications!**